The No Salt,
No Sugar, No Fat,
No Apologies
Cookbook

THE NO SALT, NO SUGAR, NO FAT, NO APOLOGIES COOKBOOK

Marcia Sabaté Williams

Foreword by Ilene Pritikin
Edited by Andrea Chesman

THE CROSSING PRESS / Freedom, California 95019

• ACKNOWLEDGMENTS •

Many thanks for helping me with this book go to Ilene Pritikin of Santa Barbara, California, who took so much of her time reading and helping me with recipes; Barbara Wellsteed, M.S., registered dietitian at Delaronde Hospital in Chalmette, Louisiana; Slidell Feed and Seed Store for help with terminology; Muriel Hubert, Alice Weller, and Margie Crosby of New Orleans and Slidell, Louisiana, and Yvette Jegg of Paris, France and Panama City Beach, Florida, for help with French expressions and phrases; Pamela Arceneaux of the Historic New Orleans Collection for painstaking research; May Devitt and the ladies of the Slidell Library for all their help and research; Charlyn Schmidt, Shirley Templet, and Wilma Dickey for inspiration and advice on certain recipes; and Andrea Chesman of Vermont, editor of this book, for being been so kind and helpful throughout.

Library of Congress Cataloging-in-Publication Data

Williams, Marcia Sabate
    The no salt, no sugar, no fat, no apologies
cookbook.

    Includes index.
    1. Salt-free diet—Recipes.   2. Sugar-free diet—
Recipes.   3. Low-fat diet—Recipes.   I. Title.
RM237.8.W55 1986   641.5'63   86-16786
ISBN 0-89594-208-9
ISBN 0-89594-207-0 (pbk.)

*This book is dedicated to my husband Ray, who has daily eaten
all my experimental cooking without batting an eye,
and to Ilene Pritikin and the late Nathan Pritikin,
whose diet has improved Ray's health so much.*

• Contents •

• Foreword •

Just when I'd concluded that about everything possible that is original has been done with the Pritikin diet, along comes Creole-cook Marcia Sabaté Williams from New Orleans with her impressive array of recipes. Some of them use strictly regional ingredients, like catfish or alligator meat. You'd think that this would work to disqualify the book for a cook living in Boston, for example. No such thing. Marcia is not only an extremely talented cook with a gift for making things clear, but she has a delicious sense of humor and a penchant for exploring cultural, botanical, and other related details that make it plain fun to read.

The fact of the matter is that the great majority of the recipes will be of interest to cooks everywhere who love good tasting food in variety and want to follow Pritikin guidelines in order to achieve better health. As so many people everywhere are learning, it's no fun (and plain stupid) to be eating wonderful-tasting food if your head tells you that you are doing yourself in with each biteful.

I could easily spend the rest of my life cooking only from Marcia's book. There are recipes in every category — soups, salads, main dishes, breakfast foods, desserts, and snacks — and they are thoroughly appealing. I've tested quite a number and have been delighted with them, both for the clarity of Marcia's directions and the great results obtained. Using Marcia's recipes, you can follow a very strict Pritikin diet such as we use at the Pritikin Longevity Centers (our regression diet), or a diet that is more liberal in its intake of animal foods — fish and seafood, poultry, and red meat (known as the Pritikin maintenance diet). You can use her book to design for yourself a weight-loss diet, or a weight-maintenance diet. The recipe collection is very versatile.

It is exciting and gratifying to me that Pritikin diet concepts are reaching an ever-wider audience and that cookbook writers like Marcia Sabaté Williams are using their talents to make an exceptionally good-tasting, healthful cuisine.

Ilene Pritikin
Santa Barbara, California

• PREFACE •

I don't know about you, but my husband was killing himself. He weighed 236 pounds and is only five foot six inches tall. I prayed for his health. I even made a novena.

One day, he realized how sick he was getting because he put himself in the hospital for a check-up and to learn how to eat sensibly. The hospital put him on the Pritikin diet for his nine-day stay. There were talks at the hospital every day about how the body works, and how we can foul it all up by eating the wrong things.

I didn't think my husband would be able to stay on the diet they gave him because it meant eating no salt, no sugar, no honey, no fat — not even polyunsaturated oils — no caffeine, and no alcohol; avoiding refined foods, preservatives, and saccharin; and no smoking. A person might as well be dead, right?

I was horrified of the idea of cooking without salt. I am from New Orleans and we New Orleanians go in for very rich and tasty food. And without adding salt, how could I ever make things taste good?

It was hard to cook and eat on this diet. It forced me into a whole new way of thinking about cooking and tasting. I went to classes and to the cooking school with my husband, though I really didn't think I could go through with this new way of cooking and thinking.

In nine days, though, my husband lost nine pounds. His cholesterol and triglyceride levels were reduced to half of what they were, and his blood pressure had lowered considerably — just by avoiding salt, sugar, fat, and cholesterol. I was impressed.

I got hold of myself and said, "Look here, Marcia. You want to hold on to this guy, don't you? Well, you will just have to make that no-salt, no-sugar, and no-fat food taste good. And you are going to eat it too, because, obviously, it's got to be good for you too."

But while Ray was still in the hospital, I went to a tea. I made up my mind not to eat things that had sugar, salt, fat, alcohol, or caffeine in them. I almost went into shock when I looked at the food. Mind you, by this time I was brainwashed by lectures at the hospital and was firmly against all the offending foods. What do you think they had at the tea? Fruit juice? Are you kidding? When was the last time you found fruit juice at a tea or party? They had wine. Couldn't have that. What about cheese straws? Nope. They were loaded with fat and salt. Cookies? You know better. Cake? The same. What about sandwiches? No, they had salt and mayonnaise (fat). Unfortunately, they didn't even have a fresh vegetable or fruit tray; but even if they had, I wouldn't have been able to eat the dip.

I was shaken. How were we going to live in this hostile world? Here is this stuff that is killing you, and everyone is serving it everywhere you go. I didn't know how Ray and I were going to handle this. We both love to go to parties and love to eat out.

The first week Ray was home from the hospital, we turned down two invitations. We felt depressed. The second week we accepted one invitation to a cocktail party and turned down an invitation to dinner another night that weekend. Ray promised to drink only diet drinks, which are not allowed on the Pritikin diet because of the saccharin; but a few diet drinks are less harmful than booze. He also promised to eat only vegetables or fruit.

But did he keep his promise? No, he did not. I didn't do too well either. We both tasted the oyster patties, drank highballs, and ate all that wonderful tasting goop. Well, not too much. We ate less of it than usual.

The next day Ray did not lose his usual pound, but he did not gain weight either. The rest of the week he was good. He also walked for a half hour a day. He was supposed to walk for an hour; but for a person who never exercised because he hated it, a half hour a day was fine.

The reason for the exercise was to keep his metabolism up. The doctors explained that when a person diets, the body loses weight quickly at first; but after a while a defense mechanism sets in. The body says to itself, "Hey, I'm starving! I've got to do something or I'll die!" So, what the body does is lower its metabolism to keep from starving; as a result you do not need as much food to maintain the same weight. However, you can fool your body by exercise. If you exercise while dieting, the body does not lower its metabolism, and you will continue to lose weight quickly.

Even though he attended at least one party a weekend, and ate and drank things he shouldn't have, and even though he had a martini some nights at home, and even though he ate out in a restaurant at least once every two weeks, (not Pritikin food and including bread and butter), Ray lost 45 pounds between February 16, the day after the New Orleans Mardi Gras when he went in the hospital, and May 16. Does he look and feel better? Yes, tremendously so. All his clothes are falling off. He buys new ones and soon they fall off, too.

Oh, I guess you're wondering about me. No, I'm not overweight, and I don't have anything wrong with me. I stand 5 foot 4-1/2 inches and I weigh 120 as a rule. If I see my weight go over 120, I diet religiously for a few days to get rid of the extra weight. I've never used any kind of crash diet and I have always made sure I was getting foods from each food group: dairy, starches, meats, and vegetables. Yes, I do eat the same foods as my husband, and I love the subtle taste food has without the salt.

My kids? They will eat anything as long as it is chicken, meat balls and spaghetti, or hamburgers. Yes, cooked the Pritikin way. Forget eggplant. Of course, I am kidding to some extent. They will eat a piece of lettuce now and then or some green peas or green beans. What surprises me is they love my New Orleans Style Seafood Gumbo. They also love my Tacos, and my Egg Rolls. They like just about everything they liked before I started cooking the Pritikin way. I don't buy cookies or cake, so if they want something sweet, they have to eat fruit. That is nothing new to them, though, I never did buy cookies or candy.

I know you are probably afraid that your life is going to be difficult from now on, but it won't. This book will help you to learn to live practically painlessly in a world full of forbidden foods.

You will have to make some changes in your cooking methods, but rest your mind. There are plenty of easy instructions in this book. You will learn to eat some new foods, but you will find plenty of dishes in this book that I would be willing to bet are among your favorites.

Just think about those good desserts: Cheesecake, Lemon Cream Pie and Holiday Fruitcake that are as good as any you could eat anywhere. And wait until you taste the New Orleans Style Seafood Gumbo! The Country Chicken Stew with Dumplings is as good as any mother could make.

Take heart. You are going to enjoy losing weight and getting healthy and eating deliciously all at the same time.

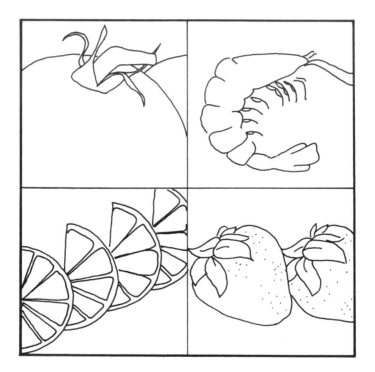

CHAPTER 1

INTRODUCTION TO THE PRITIKIN DIET PLAN

I GUESS YOU'RE WONDERING WHAT THE PRITIKIN DIET IS.

The Pritikin diet plan is a heathful diet plan that primarily means limiting animal foods and fats in order to reduce cholesterol and fat intake. Salt is limited and refined sugar is eliminated. It was developed by Nathan Pritikin, an inventor with close to 50 patents in chemistry, physics, and electronics. Following a lifetime of personal interest in medicine and medical research, Pritikin became a nationally known nutrition expert and creator of a revolutionary diet and exercise program. This book is an outgrowth of my husband's success on the Pritikin diet and exercise plan and the recipes I created to help him stay on his diet.
ed to help him stay on his diet.

For Pritikin, what began as an interest in medicine as a hobby developed into an all-consuming life-goal of changing the whole country's health. "Basically, all I'm trying to do is wipe out heart disease, diabetes, and hypertension in the next five years in our country," he stated. "The diseases belong to the dinosaur age."

Pritikin was his own first patient, when at age 40 he was diagnosed with heart disease. "I thought I was immune since I followed what everyone considered the 'Good American Diet'," Pritikin recalled. "Eggs every morning, lobster Newburg or other rich dishes every day. At that time, in 1955, physicians weren't aware of the relationship between nutrition and disease. I was instructed to cut out all activity and take medications. And I only got worse. It took me two years of research to convince myself my diet was at fault."

For over 25 years, Pritikin followed a diet and exercise program that resulted from his extensive research in the fields of nutrition, exercise, and degenerative diseases. At age 65, Pritikin's health was better than ever; at 5 feet 8 inches, he weighed 136 pounds, his cholesterol level remained at 100 (after a high of 300), and he vigorously ran 25 miles a week.

Mr. Pritikin was a member of California Governor Edmund G. Brown's Council of Wellness and Fitness and he participated in hearings of the Senate Labor and Human Resources Subcommittee on Health and Scientific Research.

Nathan, with his wife Ilene's assistance, wrote several fine books about their diet and way of life. The diet is simple, even though it seems complicated. It can be used as a diet to gain, maintain, or lose weight, as well as to become healthy.

If you wish to lose weight with this diet plan, you will eat only 800, 1,000, or 1,200 calories a day, less than than the amount of calories it would ordinarily take to support you. You are then on a Pritikin weight-loss diet. If you are eating 2,000 calories or so a day, which is about normal, but you are still eating good nutritious food that is salt-free, sugar-free, and fat-free, you are on normal calorie Pritikin diet. People who have symptoms of angina or high blood pressure are often put on a *regression diet*, which is low in cholesterol. People without symptoms of cardiovascular disease will be on a *maintenance diet*, which is more liberal in the amounts of animal foods that can be consumed.

You have to learn to count calories and be aware of how much you are eating. You will have to make up your mind to start off right in the morning. Before you get too hungry just pop a piece of toast in the toaster and spread butter or margarine on it or whatever you have the habit of doing, go to the kitchen and make your cereal and eat it. If you start the day right, you won't be tempted to say, "Well, I blew it today, I guess it's no use dieting the rest of the day. I'll start again tomorrow."

Breakfast is easy if you eat about the same thing every day—cereal, milk, fruit, and herb tea. Then you don't have to plan too much. After breakfast is the time to plan what you are going to eat for the rest of the day, down to the last piece of popcorn.

I know the planning is not easy. It takes time, but there is no way you are going to be able to stay on a weight loss diet without knowing the first thing in the morning what you are going to eat that day. If you are a night person, then plan your diet the night before.

I use a combination of two methods for planning my daily diet, but in both methods I count calories.

I have a good general calorie book plus a chart that lists different foods and their approximate calories per serving. In addition, the dietition at the hospital told my husband how many cups of this or that he could have a day to equal 1,000 calories for his weight-loss Pritikin diet. The chart will follow, but this is how it goes.

For a 1,000-calorie-a-day diet, eat six complex carborhydrate servings, twelve vegetable servings, three fruit servings, and two dairy servings. You can eat only three ounces of meat, fish, or chicken a week; on those days count the meat as a dairy serving. You can have seven egg whites a week. You can have three tablespoons of oat bran a day, if you want, or three Oat Bran Muffins without raisins. You add a few extra calories if you put raisins in them.

If you want to maintain your weight on a 2,000-calorie-a-day diet, plan to eat eighteen servings of complex carbohydrates, fifteen vegetable servings, five fruit servings (one of which should be citrus), two dairy servings (or one dairy serving if meat is eaten that day). You are allowed 3-4 ounces of meat, chicken, or fish a day, not to exceed 1-1/2 pounds a week. Limit shrimp, crab, or lobster servings to 1-3/4 ounces cooked weight per day because of their high cholesterol content.

All right, what are complex carborhydrates? Those are the starchy foods, such as beans, corn, potatoes, cereals, rice, that sort of thing.

If you look at the chart on pages 18-25, you will see how large the servings are for each item. As you plan out your foods for the day, check the recipes you plan to use, as a single recipe may contain, for example, two milk servings or two fruit servings. Check the amounts carefully.

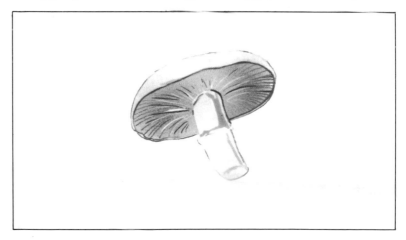

• DAILY DIET PLANNING CHART •

All of the calorie counts are approximate. They should be used to figure out servings, and not to create an accurate accounting of exact calories. A good reference for calorie counts is the USDA's *Nutritive Value of Foods*, Home and Garden Bulletin Number 72.

Dairy Servings

Each serving below equals approximately 80 calories.

DAIRY	SERVING SIZE
Milk, skim, nonfat	1 cup
Milk, skim, instant	1 cup
Milk, evaporated, skim	1/2 cup
Milk, powdered, skim (reconstituted)	1/4 cup
Milk, powdered, skim (dry)	3 tablespoons
Buttermilk, nonfat	1 cup
Buttermilk, powdered, nonfat	3 tablespoons
Yogurt, plain, nonfat	1 cup

CHEESE	SERVING SIZE
Cottage cheese	1/4 cup
Farmer's cheese, crumbled	1/4 cup
Hoop, Bakers brand	1/4 cup
Pot	1/4 cup
Sapsago	1-2 tablespoons week

Fruit Servings

Each serving below equals approximately 40 calories.

WHOLE FRUITS	SERVING SIZE
Apple	1 small (2" diameter)
Applesauce, unsweetened	1/2 cup
Apricots, fresh	2 medium
Banana	1/2 small
Blackberries	1/2 cup

Blueberries	1/2 cup
Cantaloupe	1/4 (6" diameter)
Cherries, sweet	10 large
Cranberries, unsweetened	1 cup
Crenshaw melon	2" wedge
Currants	1/4 cup
Dates	2
Figs	1 large
Grapefruit	1/2 (4" diameter)
Grapes	12 large
Grapes, Thompson seedless	20
Guava	2/3 cup
Honeydew melon	1/4 (5" diameter)
Kiwi fruit	1 medium
Kumquats	2
Loquats	3
Mango	1/2 small
Nectarine	1 medium
Orange	1 small
Papaya	1/3 medium
Passion fruit	1
Peach	1 medium
Pear	1 small
Persimmon, Japanese	1 medium
Persimmon, native	1/2 medium
Pineapple, fresh or canned without sugar	1/2 cup
Plantain	1/2 small
Plums	2 medium
Pomegranate	1 small
Prunes, fresh or dried	2 medium
Raisins	1-1/2 tablespoons
Raspberries	1/2 cup
Rhubarb	2 cups, raw
Strawberries	3/4 cup (10 large)
Tangelo	1 medium
Tangerine	1 large
Watermelon	3/4 cup

FRUIT JUICES, UNSWEETENED	SERVING SIZE
Apple juice	1/3 cup
Apple juice, frozen concentrate	1 tablespoon

Grape juice	1/4 cup
Grapefruit juice	1/2 cup
Lemon juice	1/2 cup
Lime juice	1/2 cup
Orange juice	1/2 cup
Orange juice, frozen concentrate	1-1/2 tablespoons
Passion fruit juice	1/3 cup
Pineapple juice	1/3 cup
Pineapple juice, frozen concentrate	1-1/2 tablespoons
Prune juice	1/4 cup

SWEETENERS	SERVING SIZE
Barley malt extract	2 teaspoons
Carob powder	2 tablespoons

Vegetable Servings

Each serving equals 1/2 cup (except those indicated) and provides approximately 25 calories.

Alfalfa sprouts
Artichoke (1 small)
Asparagus
Bean sprouts (12 calories)
Beets
Beet greens
Broccoli
Brussels sprouts
Cabbage
Carrots
Cauliflower
Celery
Chard (1 cup cooked)
Chicory
Chili peppers
Chives
Collards
Cucumber
Eggplant
Endive (2-1/2 cups raw)
Green beans

Horseradish, prepared (1 tablespoon)
Jerusalem artichokes
Jicama
Kale
Leeks
Lettuce (2-1/2 cups raw)
Mushrooms
Mustard
Okra
Onion (1/2 medium)
Palm heart
Parsley (1/2 cup raw equals 13 calories)
Pea pods, Chinese
Peppers, red and green
Pimento
Poke
Radishes (1/2 cup raw equals 10 calories)
Rutabagas
Shallots
Spinach (1/2 cup cookeded equals 21 calories)
Squash, summer
Tomatoes (1 small)
Tomatoes, canned
Tomato juice
Tomato paste (2 tablespoons)
Tomato sauce
Turnips
V-8 juice, unsalted (2/3 cup)
Water chestnuts
Watercress (1/2 cup raw equals 4 calories)

Complex Carbohydrates

Each serving below equals approximately 70 calories.

VEGETABLE	SERVING SIZE
Beans, dried, cooked, lima, navy, kidney	1 cup
Corn on the cob	1 ear (4" long)
Corn, cooked and drained	1/3 cup
Corn, popped	1 1/2 cups
Hominy	1/2 cup

Lentils, dried, cooked	1/2 cup
Parsnips	1 small
Peas, dried, cooked, black-eyed, split	1/2 cup
Peas, fresh or frozen	1/2 cup
Potatoes, sweet (yams)	1/4 cup or 2-1/2" long
Potatoes, white, baked or boiled	1 (2" in diameter)
Potatoes, white, mashed	1/2 cup
Pumpkin, canned	1 cup
Squash, winter	3/4 cup

CEREALS AND GRAINS	SERVING SIZE
Barley, cooked	1/2 cup
Bran, unprocessed, wheat	2/3 cup
Bran, unprocessed, oat	3 tablespoons
Cornmeal, cooked	1/2 cup
Cracked wheat bulgar, cooked	1/2 cup
Grape-nuts®	1/4 cup
Grits	1/2 cup
Kasha (buckwheat)	1/3 cup
Millet	1/2 cup
Nutri Grain® cereal, dry	1/2 cup
Oatmeal, cooked	1/2 cup
Oatmeal, uncooked	1/4 cup
Rice, brown, cooked	1/3 cup
Rice, wild, cooked	1/2 cup
Roman Meal® cereal, cooked	1/2 cup
Rye, cooked	1/4 cup
Shredded wheat biscuit	1 large
Shredded wheat biscuits, spoon-size	1/2 cup
Steel-cut oats, cooked	1/2 cup
Seven Grain® cereal	1/2 cup
Uncle Sam's® cereal	1/2 cup
Wheatena® cereal, cooked	1/2 cup
Puffed cereals, rice, wheat	1-1/2 cups

PASTA	SERVING SIZE
Macaroni, enriched, white, cooked	1/2 cup
Macaroni, whole wheat, cooked	1/3 cup
Noodles, rice, cooked	1/2 cup

Noodles, whole wheat, cooked	1/2 cup
Pasta, whole wheat, cooked	1/2 cup
Pasta, enriched, white, cooked	1/2 cup

BREADS	SERVING SIZE
Bagel, water-based	1/2
Bread, whole wheat, rye, sourdough	1 small slice
Pritikin breadstick	1
Breadsticks, commercial	4 (7" long)
Bun, whole wheat, hamburger	1/2
Bun, whole wheat, hot dog	1/2
Chapati	1 (6" diameter)
English muffin, whole wheat	1/2
Muffin, unsweetened	1 (2" diameter)
Pita, whole wheat	1/2 (6" diameter)
Pancakes	2 (3" diameter)
Roll, whole wheat, rye, sourdough	1 (2" diameter)
Tortilla, corn	1 (7" diameter)
Waffle, whole wheat	1 (4" diameter)

Poultry, Fish and Seafood, and Meat Servings

Each specified serving provides approximately 60 calories.

POULTRY	SERVING SIZE
Chicken, without skin, cooked	1 ounce
Turkey, without skin, cooked	1 ounce

FISH AND SHELLFISH (.1—3.9% fat) 1 ounce serving

Barracuda	Fluke	Porgy	Tomcod
Bass	Grouper	Red fish	Trout, brook
Bluegill	Haddock	Red snapper	Tuna, fresh
Bluefish	Hake	Redhorse	Turbot
Bream	Halibut	Rockfish	Whiting
Bullhead	Hardhead	Sand dabs	Whitefish
Turbot	Kingfish	Scrod	Butterfish, gulf
Ling cod	Sea bass	Capelin	Mahi mahi
Sheepshead	Catfish	Monk fish	Skate

Ciscoes	Muskellunge	Sole Cod	Perch
Sturgeon	Crappel	Pickerel	Sucker
Croaker	Pike	Sun fish	Flatfish
Plaice	Tautog	Flounder	Pollock
Tile fish			

BEEF 1-ounce serving

Flank steak, roasted   Lean round steak, broiled
Heel of round, roasted   Lean rump, roasted
Sirloin round bone, broiled   Lean T-bone, broiled
Lean ground meat, broiled

MISCELLANEOUS

The following items may be used in addition to the previous food servings in specific amounts.

Egg whites: 7 weekly
Low-sodium soy sauce or low-sodium Dijon Mustard: 1 teaspoon each meal
Water chestnuts: unlimited
Seeds, as seasoning only: less than 1/8 teaspoon a day
Tofu, can be served as a vegetable protein in place of chicken, fish or
    seafood, beef, or cheese. One small (2" X 2" X 1
    1/2") cake, or 4 ounces, or 1/2 cup equals approximately 60
    calories.

• FOODS TO AVOID •

Fats, oils, butter, margarine
Nuts
Egg yolks
Salt: seasoned, garlic, celery, and monsodium glutamate
Animal skins
Organ meats
Olives
Avocados
Alcoholic beverages

Coffee, decaffeinated coffee, teas other than approved
Sugar, honey, molasses, corn syrup
Sorbitol, mannitol
Saccharin, Nutrasweet®
Seeds, except as seasoning (less than 1/8 teaspoon a day)

If you will notice, the list of what you can have is far longer than the list of what you can't have.

When you plan what you are going to eat for the day, figure out how many complex carbohydrates you can have, how many fruits, how many milk servings, and so on. Starting with breakfast, your cereal is one complex carbohydrate serving, your milk may be half a dairy serving, and there is your fruit serving. With the chart, you don't have to sit down and count calories one by one, just count the servings of things by sizes and that will count the calories for you. I like to have a calorie book, too, for some odd things not listed on the chart.

Know the way you like to eat your food and in what order and write them down on piece of paper and carry it with you.

I'm the kind of person who likes to nibble all day, so I stretch my list out. Here is how I do mine. I usually list only the servings, not the calories (the exact calorie counts do differ from the charts of servings presented earlier). I've included them here to show you how they do add up.

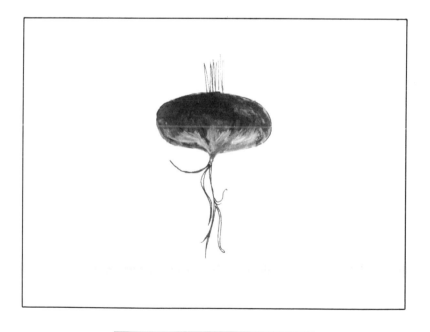

• TYPICAL DAY'S DIET •

		CALORIES
Breakfast	1/2 cup skim milk	44
	cereal	+ 89
Brunch	1/2 cup skim milk	44
	1/2 banana	+ 40
Lunch	1 cup cooked beans	70
	1/2 cup skim milk	+ 44
Late Lunch	1/2 cup skim milk	44
	1 apple	+ 61
3:00 p.m.	1-1/2 cups popcorn	+ 35
Dinner	Cranberry Baked Acorn Squash	
	1/2 squash	86
	1/2 cup cranberries	26
	2 tablespoons apple juice concentrate	80
	1/2 tablespoon cornstarch	15
	3/4 cup mashed potato	90
	4 ounces Oven-Fried Chicken Breast	+ 154
	Total	922

This still leaves me 78 calories to play around with. Lots of times I get out my calorie book and figure the calories exactly if I think I am close, because some beans have more calories than others, and some fruits have more or less calories.

Notice I don't have things like carrot or celery sticks or salad. That is because I promise myself to eat everything I have on my list. I am supposed to eat salad and other vegetables during the day, but if I eat everything on this list, I am really not hungry, so I don't promise I will eat the salads even though I should. I know if I eat what I have on my list I won't eat cookies, potato chips, or other bad things. Do you catch my meaning?

I don't promise *not* to eat certain things. I promise *to eat* certain things. The amount of chicken is more than the Pritikin program would recommend, so I would have a hard time fitting in many more vegetables anyway, but I could squeeze in some lettuce and tomatoes.

The Pritikin diet recommends eating a maximum of 1-1/2 pounds of meat, fish, or poultry a week, or about 3-1/2 ounces a day for a maintenance diet.

If I go heavy on the meat one day, I don't eat any the next. I substitute beans, or rice, or potatoes, or eat all three.

I sometimes have a glass of wine if I have calories to spare, instead of one of the fruits. I know that is not what I "should" do; but it's not as bad as eating a candy bar or a bag of corn chips.

Maybe you just love salads and would rather put those on your definite-to-eat list. Maybe you like to eat all your food at one time rather than space it out like I do. Just make sure you eat the cereal, milk, and fruit first thing. Then be sure you have the rest of the food planned out for the rest of the day so that you will know step-by-step what to eat.

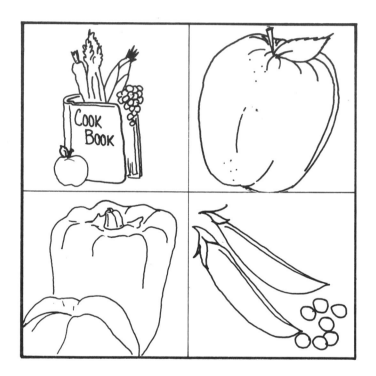

CHAPTER 2

COOKING THE FAT-FREE, SALT-FREE, SUGAR-FREE WAY

WHEN I TELL PEOPLE I COOK WITHOUT SUGAR, SALT, OR FAT, they look at me incredulously and ask, "What do you eat?"

So, I ask them, "Do you eat potatoes? Do you eat broccoli? Do you eat chicken? When they say, "yes," I say, "So do I." I used to get a little upset with the questions. I had to realize that this way of cooking is completely foreign to just about everybody. But once you get used to it, it seems very natural, and you can't imagine cooking any other way.

• INGREDIENTS •

First you must learn about ingredients that may be new to you. You will also have to learn some new techniques.

Flours and Pastas

If you really want to eat with health in mind, select whole foods instead of the refined ones. However, if you feel whole wheat flour will be too heavy for a certain recipe, don't worry. Use unbleached white flour. If you are eating all sorts of other food with roughage, a little unbleached white flour now and then is nothing to worry about. Please do use unbleached flour, though. It doesn't contain chemicals.

I don't want you to get disgusted with this no-salt, no-sugar, no-fat diet to the point that you chuck the whole thing because you don't like one whole food or another. Don't be like a lady who said to me, "I got off the Pritikin diet because I had to eat brown rice every day." That was a totally ridiculous statement to make. In the Pritikin diet you cut out lots of cholesterol and fat and limit the intake of salt and eliminate refined sugar. There is world of food you *can* eat, and you can eat some of the refined grains occasionally.

Sometimes I use white rice because I don't think brown rice will taste as good. I really don't care much for whole wheat pasta as much as semolina pasta, so I use semolina in some recipes.

Egg noodles are not permitted on the Pritikin diet because they contain egg yolk, so you will have to explore other kinds of pasta. Whole wheat pastas can be found in health food stores. Oriental grocery stores are wonderlands of exotic, delicious pastas. Two I use quite often are Toi San, or Toisan-style, noodles and imitation egg noodles. Toi San noodles are flat and have a very tender texture when cooked. Imitation egg noodles come in little packages and are very close in taste and texture to real egg noodles. Rice flakes are about the size and shape of potato chips and are nice to add to soups. Regular noodles or spaghetti can be substituted for any of these three if you can't find the oriental types I mention here.

One thing to remember when cooking whole grain foods is to cook them for the proper length of time. Undercooked brown rice will be hard and undercooked pasta will be gritty and grainy. Overcooked rice can dry out, or it can be mushy if too much water is added. Overcooked pasta gets mushy. Whole wheat pastas take about 15 minutes to cook and brown rice takes 45 minutes.

Oat bran cereal is a good form of roughage and it can be substituted for part of the flour in breads, pancakes, and crepes if you want to use unbleached white flour. It becomes very light and delicate when baked.

About Eggs

In this book you will notice that I use only egg whites. This is because of the cholesterol content of the yolks: 252 milligrams per yolk. Compare that to 28 milligrams for 1 ounce of cheddar cheese or 8 milligrams for 1 teaspoon of butter. Egg whites contain no cholesterol. Is that enough to convince you not to eat egg yolks? Egg whites contain only 17 calories and the yolks contain 59. And two egg whites will do almost anything one whole egg will do.

What do you do with all those yolks? What a shame to throw them away! Well, you don't have to. You can give them to your dog. Dogs are not affected by cholesterol the way we are. If you don't have a dog or even a cat, surely you have a plant. You can water plants with a mixture of egg yolk and water. You don't have to measure. Just add the yolk to your watering can, mix, and pour.

Salt

It's the sodium in salt that you have to cut down on, and you cannot get away from sodium just by not eating things that have salt on the label or by not putting table salt on your food.

The doctors told my husband that some salt is necessary to our health anyway. Our problem, especially on the American diet, is that we simply eat too much salt, and this contributes to high blood pressure.

In my cooking, I use a few ingredients that contain sodium or salt. According to the Pritikin diet, .75 gram of salt can be added to the daily diet. They advocate a completely no-salt-added diet only for a few people whose blood pressures don't normalize on the usual Pritikin diet.

Low-sodium tamari sauce or soy sauce are permitted on a low-sodium diet. The two sauces taste identical as far as I am concerned and can be used interchangeably in very limited amounts — one teaspoon per meal. They can be found at health food stores and gourmet shops. Some brands contain 800 milligrams of sodium per tablespoon and some contain only 500 milligrams, so check the label. Both kinds are acceptable. but I try to find the kind with only 500 milligrams.

A teaspoon of low-sodium tamari may still contain well over 200 milligrams of sodium. That sounds like a lot, I know. But did you know that three ounces of raw clams contain 174 milligrams of sodium even before you add anything to them? Three ounces of scallops have 217 milligrams of sodium in them. One cup of low-fat milk has 122 milligrams in it. Even a cup of apple juice has 5 milligrams of sodium. These figures and others, which you can find in the U. S. Department of Agriculture's *Home and Garden Bulletin No. 233* show you that there is practically nothing you can eat that does not contain sodium.

So what about the low-sodium tamari sauce or soy sauce, Pritikin bread, and a few other things that will come up which have salt or sodium on the labels?

The doctors who treated my husband said that even the people who had suffered severe heart attacks can have a few things with salt on the labels. They can't go hog wild, of course, but they can have a little Tabasco sauce. They can use a little low-sodium tamari or soy sauce. They can have the Pritikin bread and the pita bread (not the kind with honey in it). They can also use Grape-nuts cereal, which has a little salt but no sugar, for making pie crusts.

Tabasco sauce and other hot sauces can be used in small amounts even though they do contain a little salt. When I say "red hot sauce, not Tabasco," I'm speaking of the kinds of red hot sauce that usually cost less than Tabasco, and I use them in some recipes because they have more vinegar and are not quite so hot, but you get the pepper taste along with the extra vinegar, and in some cases that is what is needed.

I usually use salt-free tomato paste, tomatoes, or tomato sauce. On the Pritikin diet, you may use the ones that contain salt if you can't find ones that are salt-free in your supermarket.

You must use low-sodium baking powder in some of the recipes. This can be found at health food stores. Featherweight is a very good brand.

No Salt Substitutes or Sugar Substitutes

You won't find any salt substitutes in this book. I absolutely hate them. They taste awful. I don't use artificial sweeteners either. They could be dangerous to your health and don't taste good anyway.

You will find apple juice concentrate, grape juice concentrate, and orange juice concentrate used as sweeteners in many of the recipes. These are simply the frozen concentrated juices that you can find in any supermarket. Check the labels and don't buy ones with added sugar.

Banana flakes (also called Instant Baby Food, Bananas) are a wonderful sweetener in recipes containing milk because they do not curdle milk as juice concentrates will. They are also a good sweetener in recipes that a juice concentrate or ripe banana would thin out too much. You can find banana flakes in the baby food section of most supermarkets or the baby formula section of most drug stores. Try to use them up fast. Once the banana flakes are open, even with the top tightly sealed, they get damp and start sticking together.

Other permissible sweeteners are date sugar, maltose, malt syrup, and barley malt. I don't use any of these in my book. Date sugar can be found at health food stores, but it is not very sweet and I haven't found any use for it yet. Maltose and malt syrup should be found at drug stores, but so far I have not been able to locate any. Don't let the druggist sell you a malt syrup that is a laxative. That is not what you are looking for. Barley malt, which can be found at health food stores, contains a saccharin derivative which my druggist said is not as harmful as regular saccharin, but I would rather not use it.

Another answer to your sweet tooth's prayer is Poiret brand Pear and Apple Spread. It contains only pears and apples and is like any fruit preserve except it has no added sugar or salt. I list it in the ingredients in several dishes. I find it at many health food stores and gourmet stores. If you can't find it, write to Life Tone International, Inc., P. O. Box 1717, Boca Raton, Florida 33432.

Cheeses

It is really too bad that most cheeses must go. They contain way too much fat. I really miss them. There are a few cheeses you can use. Low-fat cottage cheese with under 1 percent fat by weight is one. What would we do without cottage cheese? You can use it in almost any recipe where you need melted cheese, such as a casserole, although it does not perform very well in a microwave. Use a conventional oven for baking cottage cheese, except when you are merely warming up a slice of lasagna or something like that.

Another kind of cheese permissible is Creole Cream Cheese which is made from skim milk yogurt.

Now, we come to sapsago cheese. Sapsago is not a brand name; it is a corruption of the word *schabzieger: schaben*, to scrape, and *zieger*, green cheese. It is a hard cheese made in Switzerland. It is green in color and is flavored with melilot, a kind of clover. I think it tastes quite good. It will keep indefinitely if kept covered and refrigerated.

On the West Coast I understand sapsago is in every supermarket. If you con't find sapsago cheese in your local supermarket, you can order it from Otto Roth, 14 Empire Blvd., Moonachie, NJ 07074. Before resorting to the mail, check very old and established delicatessens that sell things like beans and rice from large burlap sacks and olive oil in gallon cans. In New Orleans, there is a store like that called Central Grocery on Decatur Street right across from the French Market. It is an ancient Italian delicatessen. They always carry sapsago cheese. It is ironic that cheese stores in New Orleans never have it.

Keep your eyes closed when you pass the cases of cheese and sausages if you go in Central Grocery, and hold your nose so you won't be tempted to buy a muffaletta sandwich. I almost revert to type when I go in there.

I say a Hail Mary for strength and leave immediately after I get my sapsago cheese.

The only substitute for sapsago cheese is Parmesan. Unfortunately, you cheat if you use Parmesan because it has too much fat. I use just a little if I'm out of sapsago, but that isn't good to do too often.

Another cheese we were told we could use is hoop cheese. It's not the yellow kind you see at the supermarket. I understand it is a white cheese something like cottage cheese. I have yet to find it anywhere.

No Nuts to You

You won't find anything made with nuts in this book because nuts are high in fat. Too bad, as nuts would be a good substitute for meat as in many vegetarian diets. Instead, I use a lot of beans, brown rice, and some pasta. Chestnuts — regular Italian chestnuts and water chestnuts — are an exception. They are low in fat, so they are permitted.

Alcohol and Coffee

This brings us to alcohol and coffee. If you wake up in the morning and say to yourself, "I can't stand it. I hate this diet. I have to have my coffee or I'm going to die," for goodness sake, drink your cup of coffee. If it takes a cup of coffee to keep you off sugar, fat, and salt, it's better to drink the doggone cup of coffee.

Alcohol is the same. If you are having a nice meal and feel that you can't stand it if you don't have a glass of wine, drink your wine.

If you can do everything perfectly, great! But if you can't, join the vast majority. You have discovered you are no saint. Tough news I know, but that's just about everybody's lot in this life. If you can follow this diet even eighty percent, you will be and feel more than eighty percent healthier.

• SHOPPING TIPS •

While you are in the oriental grocery buying noodles, look for lumpia wrappers or pastry wrappers. There is no difference between them. Check the ingredients, though, because some have oil, or egg, or sugar in them. The only acceptable ones contain flour, water, and salt. They are great for making Egg Rolls.

Tree ears are found in oriental groceries and gourmet shops. and they are a very interesting kind of mushroom.

When you buy ground meat, have the butcher specially grind lean meat. Have the butcher remove all the fat first, and don't let him talk you into leaving the fat on because "it makes the meat taste good." You are eating it, not the butcher. It will still taste good.

All the other ingredients you will need are usual grocery store items, except for a few easy-to-purchase items at the health food store: brown rice, wild rice, whole wheat pastas, oat bran cereal, and dried unsweetened fruits. Herb teas can be found at health food stores, too.

Some recipes use commercial whole wheat bread — the kind you buy at the grocery store. Pritikin whole wheat bread, which is a brand of bread, can be purchased at a health food store. Pritikin bread is the safest to use because most of the whole wheat breads have molasses or corn syrup in them. They all have a little salt, but it isn't enough to worry about.

• COOKING TECHNIQUES •

You can't use any salt or fat or even sugar, so what can you use? People say to me all the time, "I guess you use a lot of spices." Yes, I do, but there is more to it than that. Adding loads of spices to make up for the lack of salt is not neccessary or even advisable.

One lady in our group at the hospital who experienced tasting food with too many spices commented, "Everything tastes like perfume and flowers. I can't taste the food." When a conglomeration of spices is added to food, everything tastes perfumed or Indian. A little India once in a while is nice, but every day?

This cookbook is designed to fit the American palate. However, I realize that in one part of the country people may use very few spices, and in other parts they may go for jalapeno peppers in a big way.

I hardly ever use dill. Now, if you love dill, just substitute dill for one of the spices in a recipe or add it as an extra ingredient. If there are some spices you can't stand, just leave them out.

A friend of mine from Wisconsin asked me for my recipe for red beans, a typical New Orleans dish served over rice. Later she told me she loved them. She said she used oregano, as well as thyme and bay leaf. "Good grief!" I thought to myself. "What an abomination!" I would never, never put oregano in red beans. However, she liked it. Now, wasn't that the important thing? Actually, you would be surprised how many food combinations taste great without adding any seasoning or spices at all.

When it comes to spices, you do have to be careful about your combinations because sometimes individual spices cancel one another out instead of adding more flavor.

Sometimes more pepper helps. If that doesn't work, try a little vinegar. Or perhaps 1/4 cup of a good drinking wine; do not use cooking wine or sherry, which contain sodium. Many times something sweet, such as apple juice concentrate, will help. Grape juice concentrate is even better, and it won't turn brown gravy purple, though it will tint light-colored foods purple. I haven't been able to find white grape juice concentrate, but perhaps you will, and that would make a wonderful sweetener.

I have designed the recipes in this book so the spices do complement rather than destroy each other. It would be better to try these recipes the way they are in the book first because I have measured them carefully and balanced them for the best taste — at least what I think is the best taste.

You will have to realize, however, that I am from New Orleans, and I am a Creole cook, so naturally I tend to cook that way even with Chinese food.

Chopping

The size and shape of chopped ingredients are very important. If something needs to be finely chopped, the dish won't come out right if it isn't. If the recipe says "cube" something, don't cut it into some other shape. If it says "cut or chop by hand," don't put it in the food processor.

Onions, especially, taste different if they are cut in different shapes and sizes. For Creole and many other dishes, I cut the onion in half from the root to the sprouting end and lay it flat. I make a horizontal cut through the onion;then I make cuts down from the root to the sprouting end about 1/4 inch apart. Then I cut across those about 1/4 inch apart. That is what I call chopped. If I want coarsely chopped, I make the cuts about 3/8 inch apart.

When you cook an oriental dish, cut the onion in half in the same manner, but don't make the horizontal cut. You want large irregular shaped pieces. Just cut across the round edge of the onion, then turn it and cut off another round edge and continue turning and cutting the onion until it is all cut up. The pieces will come unlayered as you sauté them and be much nicer than if you cut them square.

Putting the Dish Together

Every recipe in this book is written exactly as it should be followed. If you add any of the ingredients out of order, don't expect the dish to come out good. Sometimes you will see pepper added at three different times. This is done in order to get the flavor into each section of the dish. Take my word for it, it makes a difference.

Sweetening Instead of Salting

I mentioned before that you can sweeten foods to achieve taste. Our tongues can distinguish only four basic flavors: sweet, salt, sour, and bitter. The other ways we distinguish what we eat are mainly by the senses of smell, sight, and texture.

When you remove salt from a particular dish, ask yourself what basic taste will be left. Perhaps there won't be one, or very little of one in many foods. This is the reason just adding a lot of spices doesn't work. But, when we replace salt with something sweet, we are adding something to wrap our taste buds around, a basic flavor. Look at the labels on some of the new salt-free shake-on seasonings, and see corn syrup listed in the ingredients. That little something sweet is what makes those seasonings taste good.

Some people swear by something sour, another basic flavor, for a salt substitute, but not me. I have found if something is really bland tasting, a little apple or grape juice will make it taste almost salty. Sometimes a little lemon juice or vinegar will balance the sweet taste if something shouldn't taste sweet, but go easy on the vinegar. I find I prefer vinegar to lemon juice most of the time. It doesn't taste as sharp. Wine, also, acts on the tongue like salt, so it is very good to add to many dishes in addition to a sweetener. Carrots help to give a sweet taste. I have included them in some recipes, even though they don't seem to belong, because without them the food would be too bland.

Red Pepper is a Life Saver

Red pepper or cayenne pepper is great to really perk up that taste. You forget there is no salt when your tongue is tantalized by burning red pepper. My mother used to say "Give me any color just as long as it's red." Don't use black or white pepper. They are suspected of being carcinogenic. Go lightly with cayenne pepper when sprinkling it on something, such as Oven-Fried Potatoes, or salad, or steak. The heat is much more immediate to your tongue than black or white pepper. Ground red pepper, such as cayenne, is finer and more uniformly ground than black pepper so it coats more effectively. I use ground cayenne and red pepper flakes, which are sometimes labeled crushed red peppers. Red pepper flakes are not as hot as ground cayenne pepper if you want to just sprinkle them on something. They cook down hot, though.

There is a Chinese red pepper available, and it is twice as hot as cayenne pepper. It is used primarily in the boiling water for crabs, shrimp, and crawfish because not as much is needed as with cayenne. I haven't used that pepper in any of my recipes here, but it is worth exploring.

Sautéing

Let's talk about sautéing. Do you need butter, oil, or any kind of wetting agent in your pan? No, not with a nonstick pan. I shudder whenever I see someone dumping in a cup or so of beef or chicken stock to sauté something. The idea of sautéing is to caramelize the sugars in the food. If you add a lot of liquid, the food merely boils or steams; it doesn't get that lovely, brown caramelized flavor that comes from old-fashioned sautéing.

I rarely preheat a pan, especially nonstick ones, before adding vegetables because these pans tend to buckle, which is not good for the finish. Moreover, I see no need to waste gas or electricity. I usually chop my vegetables and keep adding them to the pan as I go, rather than dirtying a bowl. If I had the pan preheated, some vegetables would get brown before others, and I would be going crazy trying to keep some from burning while others weren't cooked or even cut up yet.

I just get all the vegetables in the pan and then turn the heat on high. When I begin to hear a sizzle I give them my full attention. There is no need to add any liquid as you sauté to keep them from burning. If they get to a point where you think they are going to burn, they are most certainly done. Just remove them from the heat or add whatever liquid is called for in the recipe. The only liquid I ever use while saute'ing is low-sodium soy or tamari sauce, and that is only for taste, not to prevent burning.

To sauté vegetables, turn them over and over in the pan lightly; don't smash them. Stirring isn't as good as turning them over, or more or less tossing them. Onions look brown around the edges and a little bit transparent or translucent when they are done, and green peppers look glossy and develop a wonderful aroma. Celery develops a wonderful aroma, too, and it is not necessary for it to get brown for it to be done. Mushrooms turn darker when they are done. Most of the time I sauté everything with the onions, and when the onions look done, I judge the rest of the vegetables are done, too.

In New Orleans, people are used to making rouxs, which means they heat up a good bit of oil and add flour to it and stir over a high heat until the flour turns brown. A roux (pronounced as roo in kangeroo) is used as a basic thickening agent in soups and stews and sauces. It also gives a great flavor. However, you can get the same effect another way.

While your sautéed vegetables are still in the pan, immediately sprinkle flour over the vegetables and continue sautéing over a high heat, tossing the vegetables over and over until the flour that is coating them begins to smoke. Continue to toss for about twenty seconds more. Reduce the heat to low and add liquid a little at a time and stir it in well, until you have added all the liquid needed. This will thicken the sauce and taste just as if you had made a regular roux.

You can also sauté in your microwave oven without any oil or butter, too. It does a pretty good job. For one large chopped onion and one chopped green pepper mixed together in a shallow wide dish, microwave on sauté or 90 percent power for nine minutes. After five minutes, check on them and stir. If they look pretty done, (limp and the onions brownish) shorten the time by two minutes. But I don't think a roux can be successfully made in a microwave oven without fat.

How to Alter Recipes

Some recipes are impossible to change over to a Pritikin style of cooking. You will see many, though, that can be altered to fit your diet.

If it is a sweet recipe, such as muffins, what you do first is substitute two egg whites for each egg called for. Then use apple juice concentrate in place of everything that is liquid. For example, if the recipe calls for butter, sugar, molasses, milk, or anything else that will melt down or is liquid, with the exception of some kind of fruit juice, substitute apple juice concentrate for that ingredient in that same amount. In the case of the fruit juice, you might want to use it in a concentrated form in order to achieve more sweetness. Spray the muffin pan with a spray oil, but do not use oil in the recipe.

With oils or salt, it's easier. Simply sauté without oils and don't put the salt in. You might have to add other things, such as juice concentrate or vinegar, to make up for the lack of salt. A good substitute for olive oil or butter used as a wetting agent or part of a sauce in a recipe is Concentrated Chicken Stock.

Recipes with cheeses are harder to adjust. Most of the time you can substitute low-fat cottage cheese that has no more than 1 percent fat by weight.

You can usually substitute skim milk or sometimes water or stock for part of the cream in sauces, and flour or cornstarch or arrowroot for the thickening part of the cream in sauces. This is also a substitute for cheese and even butter in sauces. You won't miss the butter that much in sauces.

Some sauces in recipes are primarily melted butter and are very thin. In cases like this, a broth-based sauce is good. Look at my recipe for Baked Trout and you will see what I mean. It has the same effect as if the fish were swimming in melted butter.

Write Down Those Recipes

If you do hit on a good recipe, be sure to write it down and keep it in some kind of folder. That's really how I started writing this cookbook. Whenever I cooked something that Ray found delicious, I would write it down and put it with my collection so I could remember what I did for next time.

The way to write up a recipe is to record what you measured, say 1/2 teaspoon of thyme. Write it down, then if you have to add more, put that down. When you get everything tasting just right, add up your teaspoons and half teaspoons and cups and half cups, and you will have exactly how much of each ingredient you need.

Expanding Recipes

Many of the recipes that need to be served right away I constructed for one or two portions. Some are constructed for one or two portions because I figure you will be using leftovers or items that you have prepared ahead and frozen in small quantities. I know that many people will be making most of these dishes for just themselves and maybe one other person, because most people who are going on this type of diet are the over-forty, potential heart attack set who have finally come to their senses. They don't have children to cook for any more; or, they are young singles who are smart to eat this way so they won't become the potential heart attack set in the future.

However, if you want to cook a big batch of any recipe, simply double, triple, or quadruple it. When doubling a recipe for beans, you only need add an extra cup of water, but don't increase the seasonings.

• EQUIPMENT •

Now that you plan to go on a no-salt, no-fat, no-sugar diet you will find yourself having to prepare a lot of food from scratch.

There will be no more picking up some fried chicken or pizza and bringing it home for dinner on a busy day, or opening up a can of stew or cooking up boxes of prepared macaroni and cheese.

Granted, some frozen veggies do not contain salt, fat, or sugar. Please check the ingredients because many do contain the offenders. You will, however, find yourself incredibly bored with frozen and canned foods as they lose a lot in the translation from fresh to processed.

Bread, too, is something you will find yourself making to avoid salt and sugar. Honey is considered a refined sugar when it comes right down to it, and many breads contain it.

So, one thing you will really need to save a lot of work is a food processor. You will find yourself blessing whoever invented it. Buy one that is powerful enough to knead bread dough, even if they are a little more expensive. Homemade bread is a snap to make with a food processor.

If you like yogurt, a yogurt maker is a nice thing to have.

Another almost indispensable appliance is a microwave oven. I don't think I could survive this diet without one. It is just so much easier to heat up soups, beans, and vegetables in a microwave than on top of the stove or in a conventional oven. Since you can't just pick up chicken or frozen dinners or other precooked items, you will be making many precooked items for yourself. You have to, or you will be a slave to the kitchen. You will be cooking up large quantities of beans and soups and other dishes and freezing small portions. The microwave oven is wonderful for reheating these prepared foods.

I like to use large glass measuring cups for heating most foods in the microwave. I cook in them, too. They are nice because you can measure, cook, and pour easily from them, thereby saving washing an extra measuring cup, and a serving spoon. Soups need to go into a thermos extremely hot to stay hot, so if they are poured directly from the container in which they were heated, they don't loose their heat. I have three quart-size and two half-gallon glass measuring cups. They are easy to pick up, too, since they have a handle on the side.

I also have another set of small measuring cups, one for each size, 1/4 cup, 1/3 cup, 1/2 cup, and 1 cup. I find this handy because usually there are several ingredients to measure in a recipe, and I don't like to have to wash and dry a measuring cup for every measurement. I just toss them in the dishwasher as I go, and get another one the proper size. I have a couple of sets of measuring spoons for this reason, also.

A fairly inexpensive and wonderfully useful item is a large, 5-quart slow cooker or crockery pot. Stews, chickens, and roasts can cook all day while you are at work or play. I almost always have my slow cooker going with stock or beans simmering. You have to keep a supply of these things because you will be bored with eating the same beans or the same soup day after day. You need to keep a variety on hand.

You are going to need a good set of nonstick pot and pans. I have 2 soup pots, 3 frying pans, and 3 saucepans of different sizes. I keep one frying pan especially for pancakes and crepes, and I hide it to prevent it from falling it hands that might misuse it.

I like Silver Stone cookware as I find it holds up much better and works much better than any other nonstick kind I have used. I continue to use it with a few nicks and scratches, and the finish doesn't peel off and get in the food; but these are not pots you are going to be able to hand down to your grandchildren. Even with careful use, such as always using nonmetal utensils for stirring, they will get beat up. I buy a new set of pots at least once a year. I know that seems expensive, but one trip to the doctor will cost you more than a set of pots. Even though a limited use of nonstick sprays is permissible, nonstick cookware frees you from using nonstick sprays almost entirely.

A blender is a real joy, too, and not very expensive. They are great for making salad dressings, Mock Sour Cream, "shakes," and cream soups.

You will need a good quality food scale for weighing meats.

There are a few other things you will need, such as strainers, a colander, and good knives, but you probably have these things.

• DON'T GET NERVOUS •

Now you are ready to begin a whole new way of cooking. I know at first it might make you nervous. In fact, for a week or so you might be very nervous.

When I first started it reminded me of when I brought my first baby home. I didn't know how to use a sterilizer and many things. I didn't even know how to change a diaper. I was a nervous wreck until I got into the routine. Then it was second nature.

If you have ever spoken a foreign language, you know at first you have to translate every word in your head, but after a while the new words come without thinking. You even start thinking the foreign words first instead of English, if you get enough practice.

This new cooking will be like that. Instead of reaching for sugar automatically, you won't think twice about reaching for apple juice concentrate.

Take a positive attitude and think of what you *can* eat; don't think of what you *can't* eat. Be creative with the things you are allowed. You will find you can take recipes that you like and rearrange them, and they will taste very close to the way you are used to them.

You won't be sorry. Ray hasn't had to take a blood pressure pill in years. He had been having to take them for six years before he started his diet. His blood pressure stays around 120 over 72. It's marvelous. It's worth it all to see him alive, at home, at work, or sailing in our boat — alive.

From my own point of view, I can tell you that this way of eating is good for everyone. You don't have to be sick to eat this healthy way.

CHAPTER 3

BREAKFAST FOODS, MUFFINS, AND BREADS

I WAS AT A PARTY THE OTHER NIGHT TALKING TO A GOOD friend about cooking without salt, sugar, and fat. She asked me, "Well, what do you put on your toast in the morning?"

I thought for a minute and answered, "You could put on Poiret Pear and Apple Spread, which is all fruit and no sugar."

She replied, "I don't like that. I've tried that before."

She had caught me off guard. But when I got to thinking about it, I realized the reason I didn't come up with a very good answer is because when you are on this type of diet, you hardly ever eat toast to begin with.

Mainly you eat cereals such as shredded wheat, hot cracked wheat, and even hot oatmeal with milk. Southerners like grits, which are nice with a tablespoon or two of roast beef gravy over them (see the recipes for gravy, pages 228-231). This is reminiscent of grillades (gree-ahds) and grits, an old New Orleans recipe in which round steak is cut into two-inch squares and stewed in onions and brown gravy. The grillades are poured over the grits for a favorite New Orleans breakfast.

To cook cereals, just read the directions on the boxes, but leave out any salt or butter they might require. For sweetness add your fruit directly to the cereal. You will eat fresh fruit, which is preferred to juice, because of its roughage content. Herb tea is fine to drink.

You will definitely lose weight faster if you stick to the cereal, milk, fruit, herb tea combination.

Once or twice a week you might vary your diet with one of the recipes in this chapter, but don't go overboard. One pancake please, or two pieces of French toast. Don't forget that Cherry Glaze, or Fruit Patrician have to be considered a fruit serving depending on how much you use of it. One half of the Applesauce-Raisin Topping recipe in this book contains 90 calories. One-fourth of the recipe would be just about one fruit serving, equal to about 45 calories. I recommend using one-quarter cup or less over a pancake or French toast if you want to save some fruit calories for later. One half cup of Cherry Glaze or one-half cup of Fruit Patrician is good.

Breads are not the best choice for breakfat as a rule, but the Whole Wheat Raisin Muffins plus a glass of milk and some fruit and herb tea would be great, since the muffins are sweet and moist and need no spread.

A slice of the Whole Wheat Bread spread with Creole Cream Cheese would be delicious, along with herb tea and fruit. Use the cream cheese instead of milk.

Oat Bran Bread is a good all-purpose bread; toasted and spread with Poiret Pear and Apple Spread, along with milk and herb tea, would make a nice change for breakfast.

FRENCH TOAST

• • • • • • • • • • • • • • • • • • •

Yield: 2 servings

2 egg whites
1/2 cup skim milk
4 slices Whole Wheat Bread (page 52) or Oat Bran Bread (page 53)

Thoroughly mix the egg whites with the milk. Place 1 slice of bread in the mixture at a time and pierce with a fork to distribute the liquid evenly through the bread. Turn over and pierce the other side.

Heat a nonstick frying pan over medium heat for a few minutes and "fry" each slice of toast, turning once when the first side is brown. It is finished when both sides are brown. Top with Applesauce-Raisin Topping (page 48) or Cherry Glaze (page 223).

Note: If you should decide to use commercial bread, use 2 slices, since they are about twice the size of homemade bread.

WHOLE WHEAT PANCAKES

• • • • • • • • • • • • • • • • • •

Yield: 7-8 servings (7-8 large or 4-16 small pancakes)

2 egg whites
2 1/2 cups skim milk
2 cups whole wheat flour
1 tablespoon low-sodium baking powder
2 sliced bananas or 2 cups blueberries (optional)

In a large mixing bowl or blender, lightly beat the egg whites. Add the milk and beat together. Add the flour and the baking powder and mix well.

Place a nonstick frying pan over a medium heat to preheat the pan just a little. To make large pancakes, pour a circle about 5 inches wide into the pan, then tilt the pan in all directions; the batter on top will drip over the sides and widen the pancake. If you want bananas or blueberries in your pancakes, sprinkle about 1/4 cup of banana slices or blueberries on top of the pancake now. As soon as the pancake has little bubbles popping all over, turn it over. Let it cook a little on the other side until you can see it has turned brown. Peep under the edge to see. Remove it to a warm plate.

Be sure to scrape out any crusty leavings before pouring the next pancake. If the pancakes begin to smoke a lot, reduce the heat. If they begin to stick, pour a little cooking oil on a paper towel, wet the paper towel, and ring it out. Wipe the pan with it. Repeat every third pancake. Don't worry, it's legal.

Top with Applesauce-Raisin Topping (page 48), Fruit Patrician (page 222), or Cherry Glaze (page 223).

You can double this recipe and freeze the extras. Place plastic wrap between each pancake to freeze. Reheat frozen pancakes in a microwave oven for about 1 minute. Or heat on an ovenproof dinner plate in a preheated oven at 350 degrees F. for 5-6 minutes or on a piece of aluminum foil in a toaster oven for 3-4 minutes.

Variation:

Waffles. To make waffles, use the same batter as pancakes. Use a nonstick waffle iron, and follow the manufacturer's directions. Extra waffles can be frozen.

APPLESAUCE-RAISIN TOPPING

Yield: 4 servings

3/4 cups unsweetened applesauce
1/4 cup raisins 1 teaspoon cinnamon

In a blender, combine the applesauce, raisins, and cinnamon. Process until the raisins are completely pureed.

Microwave Directions

Heat in the microwave for 1 minute on high (longer if the applesauce is chilled) in a container that holds at least 2 cups.

Stove Top Directions

Warm in a saucepan on top of the stove on a low heat for a few minutes. Stir occasionally.

OMELET CHARLYN

Yield: 1 serving

2 egg whites
1 teaspoon skim milk
1/4 cup chopped green or cooking onions
1/4 cup chopped green pepper
1/4 cup chopped tomato
1/4 cup chopped mushrooms (optional)
1 teaspoon low sodium tamari or soy sauce (optional)
Cayenne pepper

Beat the egg whites with the milk; set aside.

Place the vegetables in a nonstick pan. Turn the heat on high and sauté, stirring continuously. When they begin to cook a little, add the tamari or soy sauce. Continue stirring. When the vegetables are fairly limp and the onions look somewhat transparent, sprinkle on a little cayenne. Stir again. Reduce the heat to medium.

Pour the beaten egg whites over the vegetables. When the eggs set a little, push all the ingredients towards the center of the pan. Continue to cook on medium heat. Turn over and cook until the eggs are done. Sprinkle with more cayenne, if desired. Serve on top of whole wheat toast or with toast on the side.

HASH BROWN POTATOES

Yield: 4-5 servings

2 large uncooked Irish potatoes
1 large white onion, coarsely chopped
Cayenne pepper

Peel the potatoes, then grate. Mix with the onion and spread evenly in a nonstick frying pan. Sprinkle lightly with cayenne. Place over medium heat. Do not stir or cover. When the potatoes are brown on the bottom (peep carefully under them to see), turn the whole thing over and cook the other side. If you can't turn them over whole, divide into 4 or 5 sections and turn each section over separately. Sprinkle with more pepper and cook until the other side is brown. Serve immediately.

WHOLE WHEAT RAISIN MUFFINS

Yield: 12 muffins

1-1/2 cups whole wheat flour
1 cup unbleached all-purpose flour
1 teaspoon baking soda
2 teaspoons low-sodium baking powder
1-1/4 cups plus 2 tablespoons apple juice concentrate
2 egg whites, beaten
3/4 cup raisins

Combine the flours, baking soda, baking powder, juice concentrate, and eggs. Mix well. Fold in the raisins. Fill regular-size nonstick muffin cups three-quarters full. Bake in a preheated 400 degree F. oven for 15-20 minutes until brown.

Let cool for about 5 minutes after baking and then turn them out on a wire cake rack to finish cooling.

Extra muffins can be frozen in a plastic bag. Remove the muffins one at a time, as needed. Defrost at room temperature or pop them in the microwave for a minute or so.

OAT BRAN MUFFINS

• • • • • • • • • • • • • • • • • • • •

Yield: About 40 muffins

What the heck is oat bran? Well, it is this extremely boring, white, fine, flaky cereal that is good for you to eat if you haven't been following your diet. If you have not been eating a lot of cholesterol and have been getting your roughage from vegetables, fruits, and cereals you really do not need bran.

Oat bran is helpful since it is almost pure roughage and it absorbs cholesterol as it goes into the intestines; that way the body eliminates most of the cholesterol from the body before it even gets a chance to be absorbed.

My husband likes to eat these little muffins as snacks. He gets three of them a day even if he has been perfect, just because he likes them.

The only places I have found oat bran cereal are in health food stores and gourmet shops.

2-1/2 cups oat bran cereal
1-1/4 cups plus 2 tablespoons apple juice or grape juice concentrate
1 tablespoon low-sodium baking powder
4 egg whites, beaten
1/2 cup raisins or more (optional)

Mix together the oat bran, juice concentrate, baking powder, and egg whites. Fold in the raisins.

Spray miniature muffin cups (found at gourmet kitchen equipment stores) with nonstick spray, if you don't have the nonstick pans.

Pour the batter into the miniature muffin pans. Leave a little room in each cup for the muffin to rise. Bake in a preheated 425 degree F. oven for 15-17 minutes, or until golden brown.

Remove from oven and let the muffins sit in the pans for about 10 minutes, then turn them out on paper towels to cool further. The towels absorb the oil from the nonstick spray.

Extra muffins can be stored in the freezer in a plastic bag. Remove the muffins one at a time for snacks. Defrost at room temperature or in the microwave for 5-10 seconds.

FRENCH ROLLS

• • • • • • • • • • • • • • • • • • • •

Yield: About 20 rolls

1/4 cup grape juice concentrate
1 cup warm water
1 package or 1 tablespoon of dry baker's yeast
2 cups unbleached flour
2 cups whole wheat flour

Combine the juice concentrate and warm water. The mixture should feel just warm to your finger. Add the yeast and stir until it dissolves. Put in a warm place for 5-10 minutes.

Place the flour in a food processor fitted with the plastic dough blade. Pour the yeast mixture in all at once and process until the dough is formed. If the mixture seems dry and won't form a ball, add up to 1/4 cup water, a little at a time, until the mixture is moist and forms a ball. Turn off the processor.

By hand, you should mix the dough in a bowl. If the dough does not pick up all the flour, add up to 1/4 cup warm water. Knead the dough on a large board until the dough is elastic and smooth. Flour the board only if the dough is sticky. Kneading should take about 10 minutes. The dough should bounce back when you poke it with your finger.

Dust the inside of a ziplock-type plastic bag with flour; place the dough inside. Squeeze out all the air and zip tightly. Set the dough in a warm place to rise until double in bulk, about 1-1/2 hours.

Open the bag and place it on a counter. Beat on it until the dough is all punched down and flat. Break off pieces of the dough about the size of golf balls and roll between your palms to form balls. Place them about 2 inches apart on 2 nonstick cookie sheets or regular cookie sheets that have been sprayed with nonstick spray. Set the cookie sheets uncovered in a warm spot for about 20 minutes.

After 20 minutes the balls will have doubled in size. Bake in a preheated 450 degree F. oven for 15 minutes. Check after 10 minutes. When the rolls look brown, they are done. Cool on the cookie sheets. Freeze in plastic bags. Defrost at room temperature, or pop one in the microwave oven on high for about 30 seconds, or place in a preheated 450 degree F. for 4-5 minutes.

WHOLE WHEAT BREAD

Yield: 2 loaves

1/4 cup grape juice concentrate
1 cup warm water
1 package or 1 tablespoon dry baker's yeast
4 cups whole wheat flour

Combine the concentrate and warm water. Add the yeast and stir until it dissolves. Set in a warm place 5-10 minutes.

Place the flour in a food processor fitted with a plastic dough blade. Pour the yeast mixture in all at once and process until the dough is formed. If the mixture seems dry and won't form a ball, add up to 1/4 cup water, a little at a time, until the mixture is moist and forms a ball. Turn off the processor.

If you don't have a food processor, mix the dough in a bowl. If the dough does not pick up all the flour, add up to 1/4 cup warm water. Knead the dough on a large board until the dough is elastic and smooth. Flour the board only if the dough is very sticky. Kneading should take about 10 minutes. The dough should bounce back when you poke it with your finger.

Dust the inside of a ziplock-type plastic bag with flour and place the dough inside. Squeeze out all the air and zip tightly. Set the dough in a warm place to rise until double in bulk, about 1-1/2 hours.

Open the bag and place it on a counter. Beat on it until the dough is all punched down and flat.

Nonstick bread pans are good; Corning pans are better for fatter, bigger bread, but you have to spray the Corning ones with nonstick spray. Divide the dough in half, shape into loaves roughly the length of your pans, and place a loaf in each one. Spray two pieces of plastic wrap with a nonstick spray. Place them over the bread dough spray side down. Then put the pans in a warm place.

Check in a half hour to see if the dough has risen to just the tops of the pans. If not, check again every 15 minutes or so until it has risen to just that height. Remove the plastic carefully and place loaves in a preheated 450 degree F. oven for about 20 minutes on the middle rack. When the tops are nice and brown, they are done. Remove from oven and turn out on a cooling rack.

OAT BRAN BREAD

• • • • • • • • • • • • • • • • • • • •

Yield: 2 loaves

1/4 cup apple juice concentrate
1 cup warm water
1 package or 1 tablespoon dry baker's yeast
3-1/2 cups unbleached all-purpose flour
1/2 cup oat bran cereal

Combine the concentrate and water. Add the yeast and stir until it dissolves. Put in a warm place 5-10 minutes.

Combine the flour and oat bran cereal in a food processsor fitted with a plastic dough blade. Pour the yeast mixture in all at once and process until the dough is formed. If the mixture seems dry and won't form a ball, add up to 1/4 cup water, a little at a time, until the mixture is moist and forms a ball. Turn off the processor.

If you don't have a food processor, mix the dough in a bowl. If the dough does not pick up all the flour and oat bran, add up to 1/4 cup warm water. Knead the dough on a large board until the dough is elastic and smooth. Flour the board only if the dough is very sticky. Kneading should take about 10 minutes. The dough should bounce back when you poke it with your finger.

Dust the inside of a ziplock-type plastic bag with flour and place the dough inside. Squeeze out all the air and zip tightly. Set the dough in a warm place to rise until double in bulk, about 1-1/2 hours.

Open the bag and place it on a counter. Beat on it until the dough is all punched down and flat.

Nonstick bread pans are good; Corning pans are better for fatter, bigger bread, but they must be sprayed with a nonstick spray. Divide the dough in half, shape into loaves roughly the length of your pans, and place a loaf in each one. Spray two pieces of plastic wrap with a nonstick spray. Place them over the bread dough, spray side down. Put the pans in a warm place.

Check in a half hour to see if the dough has risen to the tops of the pans. If not, check again every 15 minutes or so until it has risen to just that height. Remove the plastic carefully and place the loaves in a preheated 450 degree F. degree oven for 20 minutes. When the tops are brown, they are done. Turn out on a cooling rack.

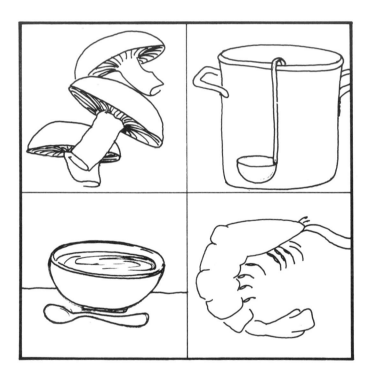

CHAPTER 4

SOUPS

I HAVE INCLUDED QUITE A FEW SOUPS IN THIS BOOK BECAUSE because having lunch on the Pritikin diet is very difficult if you work away from home. Think about it. What are you going to put on a sandwich if you don't use meat or cheese? You can't even have peanut butter and jelly. Perhaps you could scare up some sort of egg white sandwich, but if you use imitation mayonnaise, it is very perishable. A bean sandwich gets pretty sloppy after it has sat around for a few hours. I'm not saying sandwiches are impossible, but I find them hard to deal with.

Salads are hard to take with you, too, unless you have access to refrigeration. But soups in a thermos make the perfect take-out lunch.

Most of the soups here do not contain any meat, fish, or chicken so you can save your meat portion for dinner. If you wish, you could add some beef or chicken to the vegetable soup and make that your main meal for the day. Chicken would be good in just about any soup in the chapter.

Many of the soups contain beans, so it will be a must for you to cook up different kinds of beans and freeze them in half-cup portions. This will make preparing soups with beans a snap. Directions for cooking beans can be found on pages 86-87.

You will also need stocks. I make plenty and store small amounts in twelve-ounce cottage cheese containers in the freezer.

My husband takes his lunch with him every day, so I get up, start his herb tea, and go to the freezer. If I don't have any soup handy, which I also store in twelve-ounce cottage cheese containers, I find some frozen stock. I chop up some onion and perhaps peel a potato and cube it. I cook the onions and potato in the stock and then add the beans.

• Quick and Easy Soups •

Sometimes I have some leftover cooked vegetables, perhaps a little cauliflower or a little squash, so a good way to use it is to put it into a soup for lunch the next day. Look at Debutante Soup. I had some leftover Cheesy Mashed Potatoes, and some cooked cauliflower. I added some skim milk, tomato paste, cayenne pepper, basil, and some fresh sliced mushrooms and concocted a really delightful soup.

Some soups are even simpler to make than that. For instance, you can take 1 cup of cooked lima beans from your freezer, toss in 1/2 cup of frozen or fresh green peas, and 1/2 cup of water. Just heat and you will have a tasty soup. Or you can buy bags of mixed frozen corn, chopped onions, green peppers, red bell peppers, and sometimes tomatoes. Mix a cup of that with 2 cups of cooked lima beans and water enough to make the mixture soupy. Cook, covered, for about 4 minutes until the corn and onions are tender. A similar idea is to mix 1 cup of cooked lima beans with 1 cup of cooked red beans and 1/2 cup of water. For another quick, delicious soup, add 1 chopped medium-size onion and 1 teaspoon of dried parsley flakes to 1/2 cup of chicken stock. Cook, covered, for 5 minutes. Add 1/2 cup of cooked navy beans. Heat through. Top with chopped banana peppers or a little chopped jalapeno pepper. Voila! Instant soup. All these soups can be quickly made in the morning to put in a thermos for lunch.

Once you have learned the cooking techniques in this book, you will be able to create your own soups from just about anything you have in the refrigerator or in the cupboard. I do this all the time and my husband never eats the same soup twice in one week.

I suggest you buy a thermos that is large enough to contain at least two cups of liquid because many of these soups will run a cup to a cup and a half per serving.

• Stocks •

All stocks are basically the same thing and made the same way except for the brown ones. They are all the juice that you have cooked out of some meat, fish, or vegetables. They are all made by simmering such items in a lot of water for a long time, on the back of the stove.

I always wondered why people always said to simmer stock on the back of the stove. I finally found out. There was a newspaper article not long ago about a local woman who is over 100 years old who still cooks on a wood stove. Her recipes were all developed for cooking on a wood stove.

When she wanted something on a hot fire, she would say to put the pot on the front of the stove. When she wanted to just simmer something, she would say to put it toward the back of the stove. In other words, the front of the stove is very hot while the back is good for keeping things warm and simmering food.

I am finally free. I used to always simmer stock on the back of the stove just because the recipe said so. Isn't it crazy the way we do things for generations and generations when there is no need for it any more, and we don't even remember the reason or know the reason? I even simmer my stock in my slow cooker now. What the heck! Go modern!

For chicken, turkey, or beef stock, use pieces of any of these things (including the fat or skin). Start out with a very large pot. Add carrot or two, no need to peel, a couple of onions, no need to peel, but wash very well, a couple of ribs of celery, and a little parsley. Don't bother to cut anything up.

Fill the pot up with water, and if you want to be like old Granny, put it on the back of your stove, and bring to boil. Then reduce the heat way down and simmer for hours. Leave uncovered. In a slow cooker, cover and simmer for hours.

To make fish stock, use fish heads or any part of the fish. Add the same vegetables as in the stocks mentioned above. You can get fish heads cheaply at the fish market.

For brown stock, put the meat in a Dutch oven and brown in the oven at 450 degrees F. until it is well-browned. Neck bones (I'm talking about beef now) are very good for this. When the meat is thoroughly browned, add water and vegetables and simmer, uncovered, on top of the stove.

After the stock has simmered for several hours, strain to remove the meat or fish and vegetables, and cool the stock in the refrigerator. All the fat will rise to the top and harden. Scoop off every bit of it. If you want perfectly clear stock, strain it through cheesecloth, which theoretically catches any grease that is left. If you get the grease cold enough, though, you can get every bit of it off without this step. I always strain fish stock to remove any scales or bones.

Use stocks in soups; you can even put it in with beans when you cook them. It gives food more nutrition and flavor.

CONCENTRATED CHICKEN STOCK

. . . .

Yield: 1 cup

You will notice in a few recipes that I use Concentrated Chicken Stock, often in place of olive oil, butter, or margarine. It makes a good wetting and binding agent and really enhances the flavor.

2 chicken necks plus 1 back
1 quart water

Remove the skin from the chicken pieces and place in a 2-quart container. Add the water. Place in the microwave or on the stove uncovered. Bring to a boil, then reduce the heat. Simmer for about an hour. The volume will reduce. That's okay. You want to end up with 1 cup of stock, not including floating grease. Remove the chicken pieces, and refrigerate the stock until the grease hardens on the top. Skim and use as directed in the recipes.

SHRIMP STOCK

. . . .

Yield: 1-2/3 cups

Shrimp stock can be used in any shrimp dish in place of water for an even more delightful taste.

Peels of 1-2 pounds shrimp
4 cups water
1 celery rib , including leaves, chopped in large pieces
1 small onion, coarsely chopped

Place the shrimp shells in a nonstick 5-quart pot and turn the heat on high. Stir the shrimp shells and turn over and over. First they will steam, then they will smoke. When they begin to smoke, which you can detect by the wonderful difference in the aroma, continue stirring for 2 minutes, then immediately add the water, celery, and onion. Stir, bring to a boil (watch it doesn't boil over), then cook, uncovered, over low heat until the liquid reduces to 1-2/3 cups or whatever the recipe calls for. Strain. If you have a little too much, boil it down a little more. If you have too little, add enough water to make it equal the amount you need. Throw the shells away or dig them into your garden compost heap.

✳ BASIC VEGETABLE SOUP

Yield: About fifteen 1-cup servings

This is so low in calories that it can be considered a free food on most diets. Notice it has no starches.

2 medium-size turnips (no need to peel), cubed
1/2 medium-size cabbage, finely chopped
3 medium-size onions, coarsely chopped
5 medium-size carrots, finely chopped
1 large or 2 small yellow squash, finely chopped
1 medium-size zucchini, finely chopped
5 cups turkey or chicken stock
1 cup Roast Beef Gravy I (page 228) or II (page 230)
2 celery ribs, finely chopped
1 cup chopped fresh parsley
1 large tomato, chopped
1 tablespoon apple juice concentrate
1/2 teaspoon cayenne pepper
Water

Combine all ingredients, except the water, in a 5-quart pot. Add water to cover the vegetables, then add another inch or so of water. Simmer, covered, for 2-3 hours, adding water if needed. Or simmer in a slow cooker for about 4 hours.

Variations

Basic Vegetable Soup Plus. For a soup with a little more body for lunch, you can add one of the following ingredients to 1 cup of Basic Vegetable Soup: 1/2 cup cooked black beans, or 1/2 cup cooked brown rice, or 1/2 cup cooked pinto beans, or 1 medium-size potato, cubed and peeled, or 1/2 cup cooked chopped whole wheat spaghetti, or 1/2 cup cooked navy beans, or 1/2 cup cooked lentils, or 1/2 cup cooked lima or butter beans, or 1/4 cup whole kernel corn plus 1/4 cup cooked brown rice.

You get the idea. How about 1/4 cup of cooked butter beans and 1/4 cup of corn? You can use any kind of cooked beans, and you can combine any 2 kinds. If you add potatoes, cube them very small and cook for 5-10 minutes in the soup. These amounts will serve 1 and can be taken for lunch in a thermos.

FRENCH ONION SOUP

Yield: 2-4 servings

1 quart water or beef stock
1/3 cup Roast Beef Gravy I (page 228) or II (page 230)
1/2 teaspoon Tabasco sauce
1 teaspoon low-sodium tamari or soy sauce
3 tablespoons plus 1 teaspoon apple juice concentrate
5 small onions
1/4 cup grated sapsago cheese
1 recipe Mock Kitchen Bouquet (page 227)
Whole wheat or Pritikin bread

Microwave Directions

Pour the water or beef stock into a 2-quart container. Add the gravy, Tabasco sauce, tamari or soy sauce, and juice concentrate.

Peel the onions and save the peels. Start preparing the Mock Kitchen Bouquet from the reserved peels. Slice the onions very thin and add to the container. Microwave, covered, on high for 10 minutes. Stir. Cover and set at medium power or simmer and cook for 10 minutes, then add the cheese. Stir. Cover again and set on low or simmer for 5 minutes or until the onions are very tender. Add the Mock Kitchen Bouquet. Simmer covered for 5 minutes more. Taste. If the soup tastes at all bitter, add more apple juice concentrate.

Stove Top Directions

Pour the water or beef stock into a 1-1/2-quart or 2-quart pot. Add the gravy, Tabasco sauce, tamari or soy sauce, and juice concentrate.

Peel the onions and save the peels. Start preparing the Mock Kitchen Bouquet from the reserved peels. Slice the onions very thin and add to the pot. Cover and bring to a boil. Reduce the heat to medium and cook, covered, for 10 minutes, then add cheese. Stir. Simmer, covered, for 5-6 minutes, or until the onions are very tender. Add the Mock Kitchen Bouquet. Simmer for 5 minutes more. Taste. If the soup tastes at all bitter, add more apple juice concentrate.

Place a slice of toasted or fresh bread in each bowl, pour the soup over, and serve. This makes 2 large bowls of soup or 4 small ones.

EGG DROP SOUP

• • • • • • • • • • • • • • • • • • • •

Yield: 1 serving

This recipe calls for rice flakes, which are hard and dry like any raw pasta. Each flake is about the size of a potato chip and about as thin. Leave them whole for cooking. If you can't find rice flakes at your oriental grocery or gourmet store, use Toi San noodles, which can be found at oriental groceries. They are flat and about as long as wide egg noodles. Break them up and measure out 2 tablespoons. If you can't find either, use 2 tablespoons noodles or 2 tablespoons broken spaghetti.

7-8 uncooked rice flakes
3-4 green onions or 1 small white onion, chopped
1 cup turkey or chicken stock
1-1/2 cups water
1/4 teaspoon dried parsley
1/8 teaspoon cayenne pepper
1 egg white
1/2 teaspoon apple juice concentrate

In an uncovered 1-1/2-quart pot over high heat, cook the rice flakes and onions in the stock and liquid until the water reduces to about 1 cup. A little more is okay. This takes 9-10 minutes. Add the parsley, cayenne, egg white, and juice concentrate. Cook for about 30 seconds more, or until the egg turns white. Pour into a thermos for lunch.

I don't advise cooking this in a microwave oven. It takes up to 27 minutes on high.

This makes a pretty light lunch, so bring along some popcorn, and don't forget your carrot or celery, and a couple of pieces of fruit, and perhaps some Oat Bran Bread.

Variation

If you don't have any chicken or turkey stock on hand but you have some Roast Beef Gravy II (page 230) or Brown Turkey Gravy II (page 231), use 2 tablespoons of gravy instead of the stock and add enough water to equal 2-1/2 cups liquid.

✳ HEARTY SQUASH SOUP

Yield: 6-7 servings

2 small white scalloped bush squash (Patty Pan), chopped
1 small yellow squash, chopped
1-1/2 cups fresh or frozen green peas
1 large onion, sliced
3 celery ribs, chopped
1/2 cup frozen or fresh corn
1 cup turkey stock (or chicken stock, but turkey is better)
Water to cover
1 cup cooked brown rice (page 233)
Cayenne pepper

Microwave Directions

In a 5-quart container, combine the vegetables and stock. Add water to cover. Cover and cook on high for 16 minutes. Set the microwave on a medium setting and cook for 10 minutes or until the vegetables are tender.

Stove Top Directions

In a 5-quart soup pot, combine the vegetables and stock. Add water to cover. Cover the pot, bring to a boil, and simmer until vegetables are tender, about 10 minutes more.

Add the rice to heat through just before serving. Add cayenne to taste and serve.

BLUEBERRY SOUP

• • • • • • • • • • • • • • • • • • • •

Yield: 2 servings

You will be surprised how good the blueberries taste in this soup. They lose their fruity quality and look something like beans. They help a great deal to make up for the lack of salt.

1/4 cup fresh or frozen blueberries
1/4 cup sliced fresh or frozen carrots
1/2 cup frozen chuck wagon style corn (corn mixed with red bell peppers,
*   green peppers, and onions. NOTE: If you can't find this with the*
*   frozen foods, mix equal parts of fresh or frozen vegetables to equal*
*   1/2 cup)*
1-3/4 cups chicken stock
2 tablespoons Chicken Gravy (from Country Chicken Stew, page 116)
1/2 teaspoon dried parsley
1/16 teaspoon cayenne pepper or more
25-30 pieces raw spaghetti, broken into small pieces

Microwave Directions

Combine all the ingredients in a quart-size microwave container. Microwave, covered, on high for 7 minutes. See if the spaghetti is tender. If not, stir, cover, and microwave for 2 more minutes. It should be ready. Serve.

Stove Top Directions

On top of the stove, combine all the ingredients in a 1-quart or 1-1/2-quart saucepan. Cover and bring to a boil; cook over medium heat for 8-10 minutes. Stir occasionally. Add more water if necessary. Serve.

NEW ORLEANS STYLE SEAFOOD GUMBO

• • • • • • • • • • • • • • • • • • •

Yield: 13-14 servings

Gumbo is a thick, delicious seafood soup served in just about every restaurant and home in city of New Orleans. The word gumbo is thought to be a combination of Portuguese and African, and it means okra. It can be made with chicken, turkey, sausage, or seafood. There are probably 1,000 recipes for gumbo, but when you eat any of them you know you are eating gumbo. If you can't get the shrimp or oysters for this dish, you can substitute fish; however, please do try to get the crabs or crabmeat. Something about the crab taste makes this gumbo.

2 pounds fresh okra
2 large onions, chopped
5 celery ribs, chopped
2 large green peppers, chopped
5-6 garlic cloves, chopped, or 2 teaspoons garlic powder
6 tablespoons whole wheat flour
2 cups fish stock or water
2 cups chicken or turkey stock
3 bay leaves
1 cup chopped fresh parsley
1/2 teaspoons cayenne pepper or more
6 fresh or frozen crabs, or 2 (6-ounce) cans crabmeat, or equal amount frozen crabmeat
2 pounds fresh unpeeled shrimp, or 2 (4-1/2-ounce) cans, or 1 pound frozen, peeled shrimp
1 pint fresh oysters and juice, or 1 (8-ounce) can oysters, or 1 (6-ounce) can clams
2 teaspoons powdered or crumbled dried thyme
French Rolls (page 51)
Cooked brown rice (page 233)
1 teaspoon filé per bowl (optional)

About the ingredients: You can use canned or frozen okra, but sometimes it is a little tough or sour compared to fresh. Also, you do not brown canned or frozen okra. And if you live in San Francisco or some place where you have those enormous Dungeness crabs, 3 crabs will be enough for this recipe. The crabs I use average 5-6 inches from tip to tip of the shells.

Slice the okra, removing the stem tips. The other vegetables can be chopped in the food processor.

Add the okra to a nonstick 5-quart soup pot. Turn the heat on high and sauté, turning the okra over and over with a wooden spoon. After a while you will see little strings form between the okra slices. That's good. The reason for this exercise is to get some of the stickiness out of the okra. When the edges start to brown, remove from the pot to a bowl.

Add the onions, celery, green peppers, and garlic to the pot. Sauté for a few minutes, turning the vegetables over and over. When they start to look a little brown and the onions a little transparent, add the flour. Keep turning the vegetables over and over with your spoon. When the flour begins to smoke, continue to stir for 15-20 seconds. Immediately add the fish stock or water, a little at a time, mixing it in and smoothing out the flour as you add. Continue stirring until you have added all the fish stock or water and all the chicken or turkey stock. Add the bay leaves, parsley, and cayenne. Cover, reduce the heat, and simmer.

Now prepare the crabs. If you have fresh crabs, ones that are alive and kicking, soak them in ice water with plenty of ice cubes for about 20 minutes. This will stun them so they can't move. Remove them from the water one at a time, because when they warm up, they come back to life. Hold the crab over a bowl to catch any liquids. There is a little "trap door" on the bottom side of crab. Pull that off. Hold the crab, eyes facing away from you. With your left hand thumb pressing down on the left back leg and your right hand fingers on top of the shell and thumb underneath, pull the shell off. Scoop out any yellow fat in the shells and add to the bowl. The orange things are eggs. Don't use those. If you are extremely cholesterol conscious, don't use the fat. But, good grief, it is such a little bit in a huge pot, and it adds so much taste. Clean off the "dead men's fingers." Those are those hairy or feathery pointed things on the crab's chest. Throw those and the top shell away. There will be some other strange looking things in the stomach. Throw those away, too. Break the crab in two at the center and toss into the gumbo pot, shell and all, including legs. With one of the huge crabs, though, it might be best to pick the meat out after they are cooked, but leave the shells on for cooking. Add any liquid you caught from the crabs into the pot too, and rinse the bowl with a little water and add that. If you have canned crabmeat, rinse it and add now. If you have frozen crabmeat, add it. Return the okra to the pot.

Add enough water to come to within an inch from the top of the pot. Simmer for 1-1/2 hours, stirring occasionally. Keep covered.

While the gumbo cooks, peel the shrimp. Remove the little dark vein from the top of the shrimp.

During the last 1/2 hour of cooking, add the shrimp, oysters or clams, thyme, and more cayenne to taste, if needed. Add the oyster or clam juice if you have any.

Just before serving, toast the French Rolls in the oven for 7-8 minutes. The crust will become crunchy and crispy just like New Orleans style French bread, and you can use it to dunk in your gumbo.

Pour the gumbo over about 1/2 cup of rice in individual bowls. If you used small crabs, put half of a crab in each bowl and serve.

If you have been able to find filé (pronounced fee-lay), sprinkle about a teaspoon on top of your gumbo and mix in. Filé is just sassafras leaves. It gives extra flavor and thickens the gumbo. Filé is not necessary to gumbo, and many people prefer not to use it.

Note: Do not use fresh sassafras leaves off a tree. According to Judith Reagan at the Division Of Regulatory Guidance in the Center for Food Safety and Applied Nutrition at the F.D.A in Washington, D. C., the fresh plant contains saffarole, a substance that is suspected of causing cancer in animals but has not been found to cause cancer in humans. Commercial filé is required by the FDA to be treated with a solvent that completely removes the saffarole.

If you used an ordinary 5-quart soup pot and have it filled to about an inch from the top with liquid, which is how this should come out, you will get about 14 one-cup servings with 2-2-1/2 ounces of seafood in each bowl. A half-cup of rice with the cup of gumbo should fit in most soup bowls.

Gumbo freezes very well. In fact, many people make a big pot of gumbo and freeze it so they won't have to do so much cooking when company comes.

TURKEY GUMBO

● ● ● ● ● ● ● ● ● ● ● ● ● ● ● ● ● ● ● ●

Yield: 7 servings

Turkey gumbo is a wonderful and traditional New Orleans solution to "What do I do with leftover turkey?"

Also, by leaving off the cover of the pot and cooking this gumbo down to about a quart in volume, you can make a delicious creamed sauce for toast. Spinkle and mix in 4 tablespoons of whole wheat flour to the reduced gumbo and cook over low heat for 6-7 minutes, stirring occasionally. Then serve over toast.

16 ounces roasted, cubed turkey meat (about 4 cups)
1 quart turkey stock
1 large onion, chopped
1 medium-size green pepper, chopped
2 celery ribs including leaves, chopped
1/4 teaspoon cayenne pepper
1 teaspoon ground sage
1/2 teaspoon garlic powder or 4 garlic cloves, chopped
1 bay leaf
1/2 teaspoon powdered or crumbled thyme
1 teaspoon dried parsley flakes
4 teaspoons apple juice concentrate
1/4 cup rosé wine
Cooked brown rice (page 233)
Filé (optional)

Remove the meat from the turkey bones before you make the stock. The meat tastes better that way. Make the stock from the bones.

When the stock is ready, place the onion, green pepper, and celery in a 5-quart nonstick soup pot. Turn the heat on high and saute' the vegetables, turning them over and over. When the onions look brown around the edges and somewhat transparent, add the stock and stir. Add the remaining ingredients, except the filé, and bring to a boil. Cover and simmer for at least 1 hour.

Put 1/2 cup cooked brown rice in each soup bowl. Pour a cup of the gumbo over the rice. Add about 1/2 teaspoon of filé to each bowl, if desired. If you serve 7 with this, each bowl will contain a little over 2 ounces of turkey.

• Cream Soups and Chowders •

OYSTER SOUP

Yield: 3 generous servings or 4 small servings

2 dozen fresh oysters and juice (or large clams and juice)
1/4 pound or 6-8 green onions, including tops, chopped
1/3 cup chopped fresh parsley
1 (13-ounce) can evaporated skim milk
Skim milk
Cayenne pepper

Into a pot that holds about 1-1/2 quarts, pour the oyster juice. Add the green onions and parsley. Stir, cover, and bring to a boil. Reduce the heat to medium and cook gently for about 5 minutes.

Into a quart-size measuring cup or container, pour the canned milk. Add enough skim milk to make 1 quart. Scald the milk. (Do not boil the oyster juice and milk together as the oyster juice may curdle the milk.) Pour the scalded milk into the oyster juice and add the oysters. Cook over medium heat, stirring constantly, until the edges of the oysters curl. This happens quickly, so keep watch. Do not overcook. Add cayenne to taste. Serve immediately with bread or French Rolls for dunking.

If divided into 3 servings, each serving will contain about 2 ounces of oysters.

MUSHROOM SOUP

Yield: 1 serving

1/3 cup frozen or fresh green peas
4 large fresh mushrooms, sliced
2 tablespoons dried onion flakes
1 teaspoons dried celery flakes
1 teaspoon dried parsley
1/2 large green pepper, chopped
1/4 teaspoon red pepper flakes
Water
2/3 cup skim milk

Microwave Directions

Place the peas, mushrooms, onion flakes, celery flakes, parsley, green pepper, and red pepper flakes in a quart-size container. Add water to just cover the vegetables. Cover and cook for 5-8 minutes on high until tender. Add the skim milk, heat through, and serve.

Stove Top Directions

Place the peas, mushrooms, onion flakes, celery flakes, parsley, green pepper, and red pepper flakes in a 1-1/2-quart pot. Add water to cover the vegetables. Cover, bring to a boil and cook gently until the vegetables are tender, 7-10 minutes after the water comes to a boil. Add the skim milk and heat through.

CAULIFLOWER CARROT SOUP
● ● ● ● ● ● ● ● ● ● ● ● ● ● ● ● ● ● ●
Yield: 2 servings

1/2 fresh cauliflower, chopped
2 medium-size carrots, chopped
1 teaspoon dried parsley
2 teaspoons dried onion flakes
2 teaspoon dried celery flakes
Water
Skim milk

Microwave Directions

Combine the cauliflower, carrots, parsley, onion flakes, and celery flakes in a 2-quart container. Add about 1 inch of water. Cook, covered, for 7 minutes on high, or until the vegetables are tender. Test the cauliflower to see if it is just tender. It should still be a little firm, not mushy. Then enough skim milk to cover the vegetables. Heat through and serve.

Stove Top Directions

Combine the cauliflower, carrots, parsley, onion flakes, and celery flakes in a 2-quart or larger pot. Add about 1 inch of water. Bring to a boil and cover. Cook over medium heat for 7-8 minutes, or until the vegetables are tender. Test the cauliflower to see if it is just tender. It should still be a little firm, not mushy. Then add enough skim milk to cover the vegetables. Heat through and serve.

CRAB BISQUE

Yield: 5 servings

No one will be able to tell this bisque doesn't have cream or butter.

1 cup turkey stock
1/4 pound or 6-8 green onions, including the green part, chopped
3/4 cup finely chopped carrot
1-1/4 cups Burgundy
1 (13-ounce) can evaporated skim milk
1/4 teaspoon cayenne pepper
2 tablespoons no-salt tomato paste
1 (6-ounce) can or 2/3 cup firmly packed white crabmeat

Pour the turkey stock into a 1-1/2-quart or 2-quart saucepan. Add the onions and carrots. Cover and bring to a boil. Simmer for about 5 minutes until the vegetables are tender. Add the Burgundy and simmer for about 3 minutes, covered. Add the milk, cayenne, and tomato paste; mix well. Rinse the crabmeat if canned and add it last. Stir in and heat the soup through.

If divided into 5 servings, each serving will contain slightly over 1 ounce of crabmeat. This soup freezes well.

FRENCH POTATO LEEK SOUP

Yield: 5-6 servings

1-1/2 cups chopped leeks, including some green
2 cups diced potatoes
1/4 teaspoon cayenne pepper
1 medium-size to large carrot, finely chopped
Water
1-1/2 cups skim milk
1/2 teaspoon dried basil

Microwave Directions
Place the leeks, potatoes, cayenne, and carrot in a 2-quart container. Cover with water. Cover and cook on high for 10 minutes. Stir. Cover and cook on medium for 6 minutes. Stir and check to see if the vegetables are tender. If not, cover and cook for a few more

minutes on medium until the vegetables are tender. Add the skim milk and basil and heat through.

Stove Top Directions

Place the leeks, potatoes, cayenne, and carrot in a 2-quart pot. Cover with water. Cover and cook over medium heat until the potatoes are very soft and the leeks are tender, 5-6 minutes after the water starts to boil. Stir occasionally. Add the skim milk and basil and heat through.

If you like, let the soup cool, then process in a blender until very smooth. This tastes best if eaten the following day. Serve hot.

CARROT CREAM CHOWDER
• • • • • • • • • • • • • • • • • • •
Yield: 7-8 servings

3 large carrots, chopped
2 celery ribs, chopped
1 large onion, chopped
2 large potatoes, peeled
2-1/2 cups chicken stock
1/4 cup white wine
1 (13-ounce) can evaporated skim milk (or 1-1/2 skim milk)
1/4 teaspoon cayenne pepper or more

Microwave Directions

Combine the carrots, celery, onion, and potatoes in a 5-quart container with the chicken stock and wine. If the liquid does not cover the vegetables, add more stock or water. Cover and cook on high for 16 minutes. Stir. Reduce to medium and cook, covered, for 10 minutes or until the vegetables are tender. Stir in the milk and cayenne, heat through, and serve.

Stove Top Directions

Combine the carrots, celery, onion, and potatoes in a 5-quart pot with the chicken stock and wine. If the liquid does not cover the vegetables, add more stock or water. Bring to a boil and cook over medium heat, covered, until the vegetables are tender, about 10 minutes after the water starts to boil. Stir once while cooking. Stir in the milk and cayenne, heat through, and serve.

DEBUTANTE SOUP

· · · · · · · · · · · · · · · · · · · ·

Yield: Four 1-cup servings

My mother told me that a long time ago in New Orleans, debutantes' mothers, aunts, or grandmothers used to give them what they called "pink teas." The flowers were pink, the mints were pink, the petits fours were pink. Other decorations might be pink too but, of course, not the candles, tablecloths, or napkins. That would be gauche.

When I finished creating this soup it turned out such a pretty shade of pink and it was so elegant it reminded me the pink teas my mother described.

This is really easy to cook if you have leftover cooked cauliflower and Cheesy Mashed Potatoes. If you don't, just cut down the recipe for Cheesy Mashed Potatoes unless you want to have some for later.

2 cups cooked cauliflower
1/2 cup Cheesy Mashed Potatoes (page 168)
1-1/2 cups skim milk
1 tablespoon no-salt tomato paste
1/4 cup fresh sliced mushrooms (3 large mushrooms)
1/16 teaspoon cayenne pepper or more
1/8 teaspoon basil

Combine 1 cup of the cauliflower, all of the potatoes, 1 cup of the milk, and the tomato paste in a blender. Liquify.

Microwave Directions

Pour the cauliflower mixture into a quart-size container. Add the sliced mushrooms. Chop the remaining 1 cup cauliflower by hand, leaving it rather chunky. Add to the soup along with cayenne, basil, and remaining 1/2 cup skim milk. Mix thoroughly. Cook, uncovered, for 14 minutes on bake or 60 percent power. Stir once halfway through. Serve.

Stove Top Directions

Pour the cauliflower mixture into a 1-1/2-quart saucepan. Add the sliced mushrooms. Chop the remaining cauliflower by hand, leaving it rather chunky. Add to the soup along with cayenne, basil, and remaining 1/2 cup skim milk. Mix thoroughly. Cook, uncovered, over low to medium heat for 20-25 minutes after soup begins to simmer. Stir frequently and cook until the mushrooms are tender. Serve.

CAULIFLOWER-SQUASH CHOWDER

• • • • • • • • • • • • • • • • • • • •

Yield: 4 servings

1 medium-size potato, peeled and cubed
1 medium-size onion, chopped
1 cup chopped or diced cauliflower
1 small white scalloped bush squash (Patty Pan), chopped (no need to
    peel or seed)
Water to cover
2 cups skim milk
1/4 teaspoon cayenne pepper or more

Use either uncooked vegetables or leftover cooked vegetables. If you use cooked vegetables, use the cooking water in this soup. If you threw the cooking water away, just use plain water.

Microwave Directions

If you use all raw vegetables, place the potato, onion, cauliflower, and squash in a 5-quart container. Cover with water, then cover the container. Cook on high for 5 minutes, until the vegetables are tender. If you use cooked squash and cauliflower, add them to warm through after potatoes and onions are cooked.

Add the skim milk and cayenne. Bring to a boil, remove from the heat, and serve.

Stove Top Directions

If you use all raw vegetables, place the potato, onion, cauliflower, and squash in a 5-quart pot. Cover with water and cover the pot. Boil over medium heat for about 5 minutes, until the vegetables are tender. If you use cooked squash and cauliflower, add them to warm through after the potatoes and onions are cooked.

Add the skim milk and pepper. Bring to a boil, remove from the heat, and serve.

This dish is even better reheated and eaten the next day.

BROCCOLI CHOWDER

Yield: 10-11 servings

1-1/4 to 1-1/2 pounds fresh broccoli or 2 (10-ounce) boxes frozen chopped broccoli
6 medium-size to large potatoes, peeled and cubed
3 medium-size onions, chopped
1/2 cup chopped fresh parsley
Water
2 cups skim milk
1/2 teaspoon dried basil Cayenne pepper

Peel the broccoli stems but do not chop. Cook in about 1-1/2 inches of water in a large covered pot until tender-crisp, about 10 minutes. Cook frozen broccoli, according to package directions. Drain the broccoli and reserve the cooking water.

Microwave Directions

Don't cook the broccoli in the microwave; it doesn't come out as good as when it is cooked on top of the stove. From that point, this it will cook nicely in the microwave.

Combine the potatoes with the onions and parsley in a 5-quart container. Pour in the reserved water from the broccoli. Add more water until the vegetables are covered by 1/2 inch of liquid. Cover and cook on high for 25 minutes.

Cut the cooled broccoli in large chunks and puree in a blender with the milk, basil, and cayenne pepper to taste. Add the broccoli mixture to the potato mixture, heat through, and serve.

Stove Top Directions

Combine the potatoes, onions, and parsley in a 5-quart pot. Pour in the reserved water from the broccoli. Add more water until the vegetables are covered by 1/2 inch of liquid. Cover, boil over medium heat until the potatoes and onions are tender, 10-15 minutes.

When the broccoli is cool, cut it into large chunks and puree in a blender with the milk, basil, and cayenne pepper to taste. Add the broccoli mixture to the potato mixture, heat through, and serve.

This soup tastes even better the second day, after the onion flavor has time to go through the chowder. It freezes very well, too.

• BEAN SOUPS •

✓ BLACK BEAN POTATO SOUP

Yield: 2 servings

1 small potato, peeled and cubed
1 medium-size onion, chopped
1/2 cup finely chopped carrot
2 cups chicken stock
1/2 cup cooked black beans (page 90)
Cayenne pepper (optional)

Microwave Directions

Combine the potato, onion, carrot, and chicken stock in a 2-quart container. Cover and cook on high for 5 minutes. Reduce to medium and cook for 5 minutes, or until the vegetables are tender. Add the beans and a little water, if necessary, and heat through. Sprinkle in a little cayenne, if desired, and serve.

Stove Top Directions

Combine the potato, onion, carrot, and chicken stock in a 2-quart saucepan. Bring to a boil, cover, and cook over medium heat for about 5 minutes, or until the vegetables are tender. Add the beans and a little water, if necessary, and heat through. Sprinkle in a little cayenne, if desired, and serve.

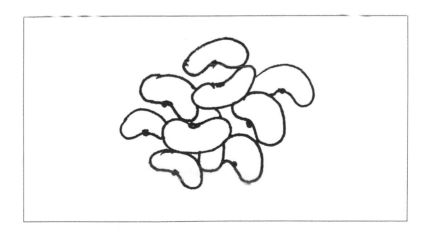

BLACK BEAN CELERY SOUP
• • • • • • • • • • • • • • • • • • •
Yield: 1 serving

3/4 cup chopped cooked, raw, or frozen cauliflower
1/4 cup chopped celery
2 tablespoons chopped onion (generously measured)
1/2 cup water
1 teaspoon apple juice concentrate
1/2 cup cooked black beans (page 90)
1 teaspoon fresh lemon juice
1/8 teaspoon cayenne pepper

Microwave Directions
Place the cauliflower, celery, onion, water, and juice concentrate in a 1-quart container. Cover and cook on high for 5 minutes until the vegetables are tender. Add the beans, cover, and cook at 80 percent power for 2 minutes, or until heated through. Stir, and if not hot enough, cover, and heat some more.

Stove Top Directions
Place the cauliflower, celery, onion, water, and juice concentrate in a 1-quart or 1-1/2-quart saucepan. Cover and cook over medium heat until the vegetables are tender, 5-6 minutes after the water starts to boil. Add the beans and heat. Add more water if necessary.

Just before serving, stir in the lemon juice and cayenne.

SPLIT PEA SOUP
• • • • • • • • • • • • • • • • • •
Yield: 10-11 servings

10 cups water
1 pound dried split peas (2-2/3 cups), rinsed
2 carrots, minced
3 celery ribs, minced
1 large onion, chopped in 1/2" squares
3 bay leaves
1 teaspoon powdered or crumbled
dried thyme
Cayenne pepper

Slow Cooker Directions

Cover the peas with water in a 5-quart slow cooker. Add the carrots, celery, and onion. Cook on high for 4-5 hours, until the peas are soft. During the last half hour of cooking, add the bay leaves and thyme. Sprinkle cayenne on soup.

Stove Top Directions

Combine the water, peas, carrots, celery, and onion in a 5-quart pot. Cover and simmer for 2-1/2-3 hours, stirring frequently, and adding water if it begins to thicken too much. Add the bay leaves and thyme during the last half hour of cooking. Sprinkle cayenne on top of soup.

• QUICK AND EASY SOUPS •

QUICK PEA, CAULIFLOWER, AND MUSHROOM SOUP
• • • • • • • • • • • • • • • • • • •
Yield: 2 servings

1/2 cup cauliflower florets
1/2 cup sliced mushrooms
2/3 cup water
1-1/2 cups Split Pea Soup (page 76)
1/8 teaspoon cayenne pepper or more to taste

Microwave Directions

Combine the cauliflower, mushrooms, and water in a quart-size covered container. Cook on high for about 5 minutes, until the vegetables are tender. Add the pea soup and heat through. Stir in the cayenne and serve.

Stove Top Directions

Combine the cauliflower, mushrooms, and water in a saucepan. Cover and cook for about 5 minutes, until the vegetables are tender. Add the pea soup and heat through. Stir in the cayenne and serve.

QUICK SQUASHY BEAN SOUP

• •

Yield: 2 servings

2/3 cup cubed white scalloped bush squash (Patty Pan)
1 cup water
1/2 cup cooked pinto beans (page 89)
1/2 cup cooked black beans (page 90)

Microwave Directions

Place squash in a quart container. Add water. Cover and cook on high for 5 minutes, or until the squash is tender. Add the beans and heat, adding more water if it is not soupy enough.

Stove Top Directions

Place the squash in a 1-quart or 1-1/2-quart saucepan, add the water, cover, and bring to a boil over medium heat. Cook for 5 minutes or until squash is tender. Add the beans and heat, covered, over low heat. Stir often. Add more water, if necessary.

BEAUCOUP BEAN SOUP

• • • • • • • • • • • • • • • • • • • •

Yield: 14-15 servings

This is a take-off on an old Louisiana plantation recipe. In the old days they used ham to season this, but with the adjustments I have made, you won't miss the ham. You can add shrimp or chicken chunks to for a nice variation.

Beaucoup (pronounced bo-koo) is the French word for plenty or lots of, so this is literally "lots of beans soup." If you can't find every single variety, either leave some out (but make up for the amount with the beans you have) or add other kinds, such as split peas or crowders.

1/3 cup uncooked large lima beans
1/3 cup uncooked red kidney beans
1/3 cup uncooked navy beans
1/3 cup uncooked lentils
1/3 cup uncooked black-eyed peas
1/3 cup uncooked black beans
1/3 cup uncooked baby lima beans

1/3 cup uncooked garbanzo beans (chick-peas)
1/3 cup uncooked great northern beans
1/3 cup uncooked mung beans
1/3 cup uncooked pinto beans
13 cups water
1/3 cup Roast Beef Gravy I (page 228) or II (page 230)
2 bay leaves
1/4 cup no-salt tomato paste
1 (3-1/2-ounce) can hot or mild whole green chilies
2 medium-size onions, coarsely chopped
1 very large green pepper, coarsely chopped
1 teaspoon garlic powder or 5 garlic cloves, chopped
1/2 teaspoon red pepper flakes
1/2 teaspoon powdered or crumbled dried thyme
1 tablespoon low-sodium tamari or soy sauce
Juice of 1 large lemon

Slow Cooker Directions

Pour all the beans into a 5-quart slow cooker. Cover with water and gravy. Add bay leaves and tomato paste. Cook on high for 5 hours.

About 30 minutes before serving, rinse and chop the chiles. Add to the soup with all the remaining ingredients, except the lemon juice. Cook for 30 minutes, until the onions and green pepper are tender. Stir in the fresh lemon juice and serve.

Stove Top Directions

Pour all the beans into a 5-quart soup pot. Cover with the water and gravy. Add the bay leaves and tomato paste. Bring to a boil, then reduce the heat to very low. Simmer for about 3-1/2 hours, until the beans are tender. Be sure to stir occasionally and keep the pot covered. You will probably have to add a little more water as it cooks. Just simmer slowly; don't burn those beans. (That's why I like the slow cooker. I can put this on at 7 A.M. and forget it.)

About 30 minutes before serving, rinse and chop the chiles. Add to the soup with all the remaining ingredients, except the lemon juice. Cook for 30 minutes, until the onions and green pepper are tender. Stir in the fresh lemon juice and serve.

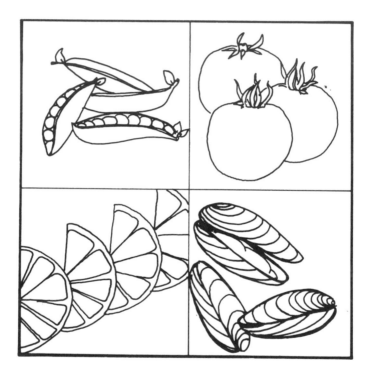

CHAPTER 5

MEATLESS MAIN DISHES

UNLESS YOU ARE A VEGETARIAN, YOU WILL PROBABLY HAVE TO reconsider what constitutes a main meal dish because you will be eating many of your meals minus meat.

Sometimes you will be eating beans, rice, or pastas instead of meat, or substituting low-fat cottage cheese for meat in some dishes. A dinner might consist of Broccoli Pilaf which has rice and vegetables, but no meat. If you limit your serving to 1/2 cup, you might add 2 cups of beans to your plate. You might also add some carrots, a slice or two of tomato and perhaps a few slices of a peaches. I ask you: is that what you usually eat for dinner? Where is the meat? And notice all the starches. You will become, in fact, practically a vegetarian.

When my husband started his diet, he could eat only 3 ounces of meat a week, including fish and chicken. Twice a week I gave him 1-1/2 ounces of some kind of meat, fish, or chicken.

After he lost 40 pounds and his blood cholesterol level came way down, I loosened up a little and started giving him meat more often in dishes such as Baked Chicken, Baked Trout, and Chicken Tropicana. But still, I only give him something like one chicken breast, or one thigh, or a rather small trout.

He doesn't lose weight fast this way, but he loses a little, and his blood pressure stays down and so does his blood sugar and cholesterol.

When you lose a great deal of weight and are tired of the strenuous diet, you might want to do this for a while. Don't go back to the salt, sugar, and fats. You can go back to eating roast beef, mashed potatoes, and gravy with vegetables if you cook them without the salt and fat. You should stay with a small piece of meat, though.

But let's get back to when you first go on your diet and you are preparing meatless meals. What sort of combinations of foods will you be serving? Here are some ideas; each of these meals runs between 450 and 470 calories, good for dinner on a 1,000 calorie a day diet.

• MEAL NO. 1 •

How about 1 cup of Cauliflower Carrot Soup for starters? Then, on a plate, place 1 cup of cooked brown rice and 1 cup of red kidney beans over the rice. This is a New Orleans favorite. To complete the soul food plate, add a cup or two of Collards and Carrots. For color add a few slices of tomato and perhaps a sprig of parsley. Always have a fresh green salad on the side with, perhaps, Italian Salad Dressing.

When you serve the Cauliflower Carrot Soup, you will want to measure it so it will fit in with your milk allowance for the day. Eat a chunk of fresh pineapple for dessert.

• MEAL NO. 2 •

Another day you could have a meal with a Spanish flair. First, serve some Basic Vegetable Soup. Then have 1 cup of Spanish Rice with 1 cup of black beans on the side. Cook up some broccoli, cauliflower, mushrooms, and carrots mixed in the same pot. Serve them on the plate. For something sweet, cut some orange slices in half and place on the plate. A little parsley makes a nice decoration. Have Cole Slaw a la Tropique in another bowl to complete the meal.

• MEAL NO. 3 •

My husband just loves Broccoli Mushroom Bake. Serve that on a plate along with 1/2 cup fresh or frozen peas and fresh sliced mushrooms that have been cooked together, and 1/2 cup of sliced cooked carrots. Don't forget a sprig of curly parsley. A cup of Basic Vegetable Soup is nice along with this and a green salad with Greek Dressing. Serve an apple after dinner with herb tea.

• MEAL NO. 4 •

A Stuffed Irish Potato is a nice treat served with 1-1/2 cups of Pinto Beans. The potato should be no more than 2 inches in diameter. The plate will be really appealing if you add 4 Mock Stuffed Egg Halves and 1 cup of steamed spinach mixed with sliced mushrooms. An added 1/2 cup of sliced carrots would look very pretty and appetizing. Can you picture the color combination? Don't forget a green salad with Italian Salad Dressing. Mushroom Soup to start the meal would be nice, if you have enough milk allowance left over. Serve a fresh peach on a pretty plate along with some herb tea after dinner.

• MEAL NO. 5 •

Acorn Squash Cheese Bake is wonderfully attractive as well as delicious. Serve it with 1 cup of large lima beans on the side, plus 1/2 cup of steamed carrots. Sprinkle a little chopped fresh parsley over the carrots. Serve with Socrates Salad. A cup of Hearty Squash Soup would be good with this. A cup of Cantaloupe Carob Ice Cream could be a refreshing finale to this meal.

• MEAL NO. 6 •

Two Burrito Wrap-Ups are great. Serve with a few slices of tomato on the side and 2-3 cups of Red Cabbage With Turnips. A large green salad with B & B Dressing would complement this nicely. Basic Vegetable Soup is light enough to start this meal. Strawberry Mountain would be a satisfying finish to this meal if you have some milk allowance left.

• MEAL NO. 7 •

Try 1/2 cup of Mexicorn and Rice with 1/2 cup of lentils combined with 1 cup of black-eyed peas on the side, plus a Baked Tomato, and 1 cup of steamed spinach. Place some peach slices on the plate. A steamed artichoke would be wonderful with 1/4 cup of Sour Cream Dressing to dip the leaves in. You can also have a green salad with Fresh Tomato Dressing. Start with some Basic Vegetable Soup.

• MEAL NO. 8 •

Stewed Eggplant — as much as you can eat — over 1-1/2 cups of brown rice is delicious. Serve with Basic Vegetable Soup and a huge green salad topped with Italian Salad Dressing. Serve a Banana Snack for dessert.

• MEAL NO. 9 •

For a super dinner, have 1 cup of Creamed Spaghetti Milano along with 1 serving of Spinach Florentine. A 1/2 cup serving of steamed carrots will add color as well as vitamins. Serve with a huge green salad with Italian Salad Dressing and a cup of Blueberry Soup. Cantaloupe Ice Cream would make a nice dessert.

• MEAL NO. 10 •

One serving of Noodles Villa d'Este, a Baked Tomato, and 1 or 2 cups of Turnips With Turnip Greens is a delicious combination. A piece of fresh pineapple on the plate would be beautiful as well as delicious. Basic Vegetable Soup and a green salad with Fresh Tomato Dressing goes with this.

• MEAL NO. 11 •

Stuffed Eggplant made with low-fat cottage cheese, a cup of Basic Vegetable Soup, Old-Fashioned Salad, and a 2-inch by 8-inch slice of fresh watermelon for dessert is a very tasty meal.

• MEAL NO. 12 •

Tree ears and noodles with as much sauce as you want to eat and 1-1/2 cups of the noodles is a change of pace. Serve with 1 cup of steamed sliced carrots. Try Basic Vegetable Soup for starters and a large green salad with Italian Salad Dressing or Greek Dressing. Serve with fresh orange sections on another dish.

• MEAL NO. 13 •

Basic Vegetable Soup to which you have added 25 sticks of whole wheat spaghetti, either precooked or cooked right in the soup as you heat it, 2 Armenian Stuffed Cabbage rolls, and a green salad with Fresh Tomato

Dressing is a good meal. For dessert have a fresh plum.

So, you see, it is possible to serve delicious and attractive meals without meat. My husband almost always says "Doesn't this look delicious!" when I serve him meatless meals. They are almost always more colorful and more appetizing than meat, potatoes, and one vegetable.

When you get through eating one of these meals, you will feel just as full and satisfied as if you had had meat.

• HOW TO MAKE A • • PLATE ATTRACTIVE •

One afternoon I went out to lunch with a friend and her husband. We went to a local salad bar. After I had placed all the goodies on my plate, her husband looked over and said, "How come your salad looks so pretty and mine doesn't?"

Mainly, I would say mine was neat. I had layered it nicely, starting with lettuce over the whole plate, then cucumbers, then I placed cauliflower here and there and interspersed that with broccoli. I sprinkled a few onion rings over that and then radish circles. Shredded carrots went over the radishes in the middle and then a dollop of cottage cheese on top. Around the edges I placed cherry tomatoes. I probably had a few other things on there, too, but the idea is that I was neat and I had things colorfully placed.

What do I mean colorfully placed? If you ever took art you probably learned about contrasting colors. Red and green are contrasting colors. Yellow and purple are contrasting colors. Blue and orange are contrasting colors. Some colors complement each other. Blue and yellow are complementary. Red and blue are complementary. Yellow and red are complementary.

What am I getting at? When you put food on a plate, first of all be neat. Then try to put pretty colors together. For instance, yellow squash and red cabbage (purple) with a stuffed potato (white) can knock your socks off, because of the yellow and purple. I usually don't stop there, though, because the potato is a little dull. Let's have even more contrast. Put a bed of curly parsley (green) and a tomato slice or two (red) on one side of the plate. This type of color combination might not work for clothes or wallpaper, but it does for food.

Black and white in food is pretty, too. Black beans on a plate is startling next to Oven-Fried Potatoes, spinach, and carrots. Of course, black beans are not totally black when cooked, but they are close enough.

If you can't figure all this color coding out, you can't go wrong with carrots. They make any plate bright. Use fresh fruit and vegetables. Lemon wedges are pretty. Raw foods usually have the most color. Watch when you go out to eat in a restaurant. Sometimes the chef puts strawberries and peach slices on a little piece of lettuce on the side of your plate, just so you will say "Wow! Isn't this beautiful?"

One thing I can positively guarantee, a chunk of fresh pineapple will make any plate look scrumptuous and it tastes the same.

Think about foods when you cook them, too. Yellow and red are the best complementary colors for food. For instance, you could cook some chopped red bell peppers with your yellow squash.

Pretty china is nice but not essential. Ordinary, everyday china can be just fine. It is the color in the foods themselves that makes a plate look pretty.

Another thing to remember is not serve two saucy things on a plate at the same time unless it is two kinds of beans, which really amounts to just one thing, beans. This not only looks better but tastes better, too.

• BEANS •

When you are on the Pritikin diet, beans are a real staple, a substitute for meat.

Beans can be awfully bland without salt, but you can spice them up to taste pretty good. Pinto beans taste the best without salt, and then garbanzos. Black beans, I'd say, are next, then lima beans.

If you absolutely can't stand the way the beans taste — if they have no taste — it is all right to add a tablespoon of low-sodium soy or tamari sauce to the pot. They will taste much better.

I try to stay away from this practice as much as possible because even the low-sodium soy and tamari sauces do contain salt.

I was used to eating red beans cooked with ham and salt. At first, when I ate them without the salt and ham I couldn't taste anything, or very little. Now I like them. I'm happy with them plain, even without Tabasco sauce.

However, my husband still squirts Tabasco sauce on beans, any kind of beans. He still misses that salty taste. He also puts chopped raw onions on beans, too, and that is a very good addition.

Another trick to make beans taste better is to mix two or three kinds together. I usually don't cook different kinds of beans together in the same pot. I make up half-cup containers of beans for the freezer. When I am ready to cook, I take one container of pinto beans, say, and mix them with limas or maybe lentils. Lentils are the most bland tasting bean of all, so I almost always mix them with other beans.

A squirt of fresh lemon juice sometimes is good on beans. You might try that. Another great thing to put in beans is lemon grass. I didn't add it to any of the recipes because it is so hard to find. It smells just like lemon but it has a sweet and slightly tangy taste. I cut it up in three-inch lengths and freeze it in plastic bags. Three pieces like that are enough for a pot of beans. It gives a lovely aroma and flavor. Add it to any bean recipe.

I really like adding a little water to a cup of beans to make soup for lunch. I also drink a half-cup milk serving. Then, if I can fit them in, I eat some vegetables. I am usually pretty full after eating bean soup and milk. Later I eat my fruit and the rest of my milk serving. The amazing thing is if I eat everything I'm supposed to up to my 1,000 calories, I really feel stuffed and I don't feel tempted to stop at a convenience store for potato chips and a candy bar.

Beans are one of the best foods for you. I don't have a recipe for every kind of bean in this book; but, basically they all taste good when they are cooked with onions, green pepper, parsley, pepper, and carrots. The carrots give a little sweetness. Celery is nice, too. Thyme and bay leaf taste good in all beans. Garlic is nice in some beans, too. If the beans still don't have taste, add some apple juice concentrate; that almost always does the trick. Then, if you are desperate for more flavor, add 1 tablespoon of low-sodium tamari or soy sauce.

Start all beans with lots of water, usually nine or ten cups for a pound. They don't do as well if you have to add water as they cook; they will usually stay hard. There is really no need to presoak beans if you cook them in a slow cooker. If you soak them overnight they might cook a little faster, but in a slow cooker, who cares? Even when I cook them in a big pot on top of the stove, I still don't presoak them, and they always come out fine.

I usually start cooking my beans in plain water in the slow cooker because if you add the seasoning in the beginning, the seasonings lose their taste. Add seasonings, except for bay leaves, during the last thirty or forty minutes.

RED OR KIDNEY BEANS

• • • • • • • • • • • • • • • • • • • •

Yield: About twelve 1/2-cup servings

One of my mother's friend's sons married a children's heart specialist from up north. The first time she saw that a young patient in a New Orleans hospital was served red beans and rice for dinner, she couldn't believe it. She marched down to bawl out the dietitian for giving the child 2 starches. The dietitian and the kitchen helpers looked at her like she was crazy. Everybody in New Orleans eats red beans and rice. It is probably on every menu in the city, and if it isn't you can probably get it anyway.

1 pound or 2-2/3 cups dry red kidney beans
2 bay leaves
9-1/2 cups water
1 celery rib, including leaves, chopped
1/2 cup chopped fresh parsley
1 medium-size to large onion, chopped
1 medium-size to large green pepper, chopped
2 teaspoons garlic powder or 4 garlic cloves, chopped
4 teaspoons low-sodium tamari or soy sauce
1/4-1/2 teaspoon red pepper flakes
1 teaspoon powdered or crumbled thyme

Slow Cooker Directions

Rinse the beans. Combine with the bay leaves and water in the slow cooker. Cover and cook on high for 4-1/2 hours. Add the remaining ingredients and cook for 30-40 minutes until the green pepper is tender.

Stove Top Directions

If you are going to cook the beans on top of the stove, be sure you are going to be home all morning or all afternoon. Rinse the beans. Combine the beans, bay leaves, and water in a large pot. Cover and simmer for about 3 hours. Add the remaining ingredients and simmer for 30-40 minutes, until the green pepper is tender. Stir every so often to keep the beans from burning on the bottom. You shouldn't need any more water, but if the beans start to dry out, add more.

PINTO BEANS

• •

Yield: About fourteen 1/2-cup servings

1 pound or 2-2/3 cups dried pinto beans
9 cups water
1/4 cup dried celery flakes
1/4 cup dried onion flakes or dried chopped onions
1/4 cup chili powder
2 teaspoons garlic powder
2 teaspoons low-sodium tamari or soy sauce
1 large green pepper, diced
1/2 teaspoon red pepper flakes
3 tablespoons apple juice concentrate
2 tablespoons fresh lemon juice

Slow Cooker Directions

Rinse the beans and combine them with the water in a 5-quart slow cooker. Cover and cook on high for 4-1/2 hours. Add the remaining ingredients, except for the lemon juice, and cook for 30-40 minutes more, until the green pepper is tender. Stir in the lemon juice just before serving.

Stove Top Directions

Rinse the beans and combine them with the water in a 5-quart soup pot. Cover and simmer for 3-1/3 hours. Stir often. Add the remaining ingredients, except for the lemon juice, and simmer for 30-40 minutes, until the green pepper is tender. Stir in the lemon juice just before serving.

Serve with Spanish Rice (page 109), mixed steamed vegetables, and a small serving of broiled hamburger or steak.

BLACK-EYED PEAS

Yield: About twelve 1/2-cup servings

1 pound or 2-2/3 cups dried black-eyed peas
10 cups water
2 bay leaves
1 cup chopped celery, including leaves
2 medium-size onions, chopped
1 small green pepper, chopped
3/4 teaspoon cayenne pepper
1-1/2 teaspoons powdered or crumbled thyme
2 tablespoons orange juice concentrate

Slow Cooker Directions

Rinse the peas and combine them with the water and bay leaves in a 5-quart slow cooker. Cover and cook on high for 4-1/2 hours. Add the remaining ingredients and cook for 30-40 minutes more, until the vegetables are tender.

Stove Top Directions

Rinse the peas and combine them with the water and bay leaves in a 5-quart soup pot. Cover and simmer for 1 hour. Add the remaining ingredients and simmer, covered, for 30-40 minutes more, until the vegetables are tender.

BLACK BEANS

Yield: About twelve 1/2-cup servings

1 pound or 2-2/3 cups dried black beans
9 cups water
1 cup chopped onions
1 cup chopped green pepper
1 celery rib and leaves, chopped
1/2 cup chopped fresh parsley
1/4 teaspoon red pepper flakes
1/2 teaspoon garlic powder
1/2 teaspoon crumbled or powdered thyme

Slow Cooker Directions

Rinse the beans. Combine with the water in a 5-quart slow cooker. Cover and cook on high for 4-1/2 hours. Add the remaining ingredients and cook for 30-40 minutes more, until the vegetables are tender.

Stove Top Directions

Rinse the beans. Combine with the water in a 5-quart soup pot. Cover and simmer for 2-1/2 hours, until the beans are tender. Add the other ingredients and simmer, covered, for 30-40 minutes more, until vegetables are tender.

Just for fun, taste the beans before you add anything to them. I think you will be surprised how sweet and good they taste. You might like them just as they are.

LIMA BEANS

• • • • • • • • • • • • • • • • • • •

Yield: About twelve 1/2-cup servings

These beans taste so good by themselves, you should taste them before you add the onions, green pepper, carrots, and cayenne.

1 pound or 2-2/3 cups dried large or baby lima beans
9 cups water
3/4 cup chopped green pepper
1/2 cup chopped onion
1/4 cup chopped carrot
1/4 teaspoon cayenne pepper

Slow Cooker Directions

Rinse the beans. Combine with the water in a 5-quart slow cooker. Cover and cook on high for 4-1/2 hours. Add the remaining ingredients and cook for 30-40 minutes more, until the vegetables are tender.

Stove Top Directions

Rinse the beans. Combine with the water in a 5-quart pot. Cover and simmer for 3 hours. Stir often. Add the remaining ingredients and cook for 30-40 minutes more, until the vegetables are tender.

LENTILS

• •

Yield: About twelve 1/2-cup servings

1 pound or 2-2/3 cups dried lentils
9 cups water
1 cup chopped onions
1/2 cup chopped green pepper
1/2 cup chopped carrots
6 tablespoons apple juice concentrate
3/4 teaspoon cayenne pepper
1 tablespoon low-sodium tamari or soy sauce
1/2 teaspoon mace 4 teaspoons fresh lemon juice

Slow Cooker Directions

Rinse the lentils. Combine with the water in a 5-quart slow cooker. Cover and cook on high for 4-1/2 hours. Add the remaining ingredients, except the lemon juice, and cook for 30-40 minutes more, until the vegetables are tender. Add the lemon juice, stir, and serve.

Stove Top Directions

Rinse the lentils. Combine with the water in a 5-quart soup pot. Cover and simmer for 2 hours. Stir every so often. Add the remaining ingredients, except the lemon juice, and simmer for 30-40 minutes more, until the vegetables are tender. Add the lemon juice and stir.

NAVY BEANS

• • • • • • • • • • • • • • • • • • •

Yield: About twelve 1/2-cup servings

1 pound or 2-2/3 cups dried navy beans or great Northern beans
9 cups water
1 large carrot, finely chopped
1 small green pepper, chopped
1 small tomato, chopped
1 medium-size onion, chopped
1 tablespoon low-sodium tamari or soy sauce
1 tablespoon apple juice concentrate
1/4 teaspoon paprika
1/4 teaspoon cayenne pepper
1 teaspoon dry mustard

Slow Cooker Directions

Rinse the beans. Combine with the water and carrot in a 5-quart slow cooker. Cover and cook on high for 4-1/2 hours. Add the remaining ingredients and cook for 30-40 minutes, until the vegetables are tender.

Stove Top Directions

Rinse the beans. Combine with the water and carrot in a 5-quart pot. Cover and simmer for 3 hours. Add the remaining ingredients and simmer for 30-40 minutes, until the vegetables are tender.

✳ RED BEANS IN TOMATO GRAVY

• • • • • • • • • • • • • • • • • • •

Yield: 3-4 servings

2 medium-size onions, chopped
1 medium-size green pepper, chopped
1 large carrot, finely chopped
Water
6 ounces no-salt tomato paste
1/4 cup dry vermouth
1/2 teaspoon dried oregano
1/2 teaspoon cumin
1 tablespoon dried parsley flakes
44 raisins
1 cup cooked Red Beans (page 88)
1 teaspoon garlic powder
1/2 teaspoon dried basil Cayenne pepper

Combine the onions, green pepper, and carrot in nonstick frying pan. Turn the heat on high, and saute' until the onions look a little limp and transparent. Reduce the heat to very low. Add just enough water to cover the vegetables. Then add the tomato paste, vermouth, oregano, cumin, parsley, and raisins. Cover and simmer for 1 hour, stirring every now and then.

The vegetables should be tender about 15 minutes after they start to simmer, but to develop flavors, this should cook for at least 1 hour. Add more water if the mixture gets too dry. After 1 hour, add the cooked red beans, garlic powder, basil, and cayenne to taste. Heat through. Serve over cooked whole wheat spaghetti.

BURRITO WRAP-UPS

• • • • • • • • • • • • • • • • • • • •

Yield: 2 servings

4 corn tortillas
1-1/2 teaspoons chili powder
1 cup cooked black beans (page 90)
Chopped onions (optional)

Microwave Directions

If the tortillas are frozen, place them in an open plastic bag and heat on high for 2 minutes. If the tortillas are not frozen, reduce heating time.

Stove Top Directions

Heat about an inch of water in a large saucepan. Place a colander over the water. Put the frozen tortillas in the colander and cover. The tortillas will be ready to eat about 2-1/2 minutes after the water starts to boil. If the tortillas are not frozen, reduce the heating time by half.

Mix the chili powder with the beans and heat in the microwave or on the stove top. Pour the beans over the tortillas on serving plates and fold the tortillas over the beans. Pour extra beans over the folded tortillas. Sprinkle with raw onions if desired.

ARMENIAN STUFFED CABBAGE

• • • • • • • • • • • • • • • • • • •

Yield: 7 cabbage rolls (3-1/2 servings)

7 cabbage leaves
4 medium-size onions
7 large mushrooms
1 small green pepper
1/4 teaspoon cayenne pepper
1-1/2 cups Spanish Rice (page 109)
2 cups water
4 tablespoons no-salt tomato paste
1 tablespoon dried parsley flakes or 1/4 cup chopped fresh parsley
1 tablespoon chili powder
1/2 teaspoon garlic powder

1/2 teaspoon dried basil
1/2 teaspoon dried oregano
1 tablespoon plus 2 teaspoons apple juice concentrate
1 (15-ounce) can garbanzo beans, rinsed and drained
   (about 2 cups cooked beans)
7 tablespoons grated sapsago cheese

Try to find a cabbage that has not been trimmed. When you are ready to begin, bring about 4 quarts of water to a boil in a large soup pot. Cut each leaf at the base and remove carefully. Place 1 or 2 leaves in the rapidly boiling water at a time. Let them cook for about 2 minutes or until they are wilted enough to bend and roll easily. Carefully remove 1 leaf at a time from the water. Drain in a colander. Repeat.

In the meantime, chop the onions, mushrooms, and green peppers. Combine the onions and mushrooms in a nonstick frying pan and turn the heat on high. Sauté until the onions begin to brown around the edges and appear a little transparent. Sprinkle with cayenne as the vegetables cook. Place half the onions and mushrooms in a bowl with the Spanish Rice.

Add the green peppers to the mushrooms and onions remaining in the pan. Continue to sauté until the green peppers get a little shiny looking and smell wonderful. Add the water to the frying pan. Then add the tomato paste, parsley, chili powder, garlic powder, basil, oregano, and juice concentrate. Let the mixture simmer uncovered for about 10 minutes.

Add the garbanzo beans to the Spanish Rice and stir together. Put about 1/2 cup of the Spanish Rice mixture in the center of each leaf. Roll up and place the leaf seam down in a 9-inch by 13-inch baking dish. Continue filling and rolling each leaf in this manner. When all the leaves are filled, pour the tomato sauce mixture over the cabbage and spread it around. Cover with aluminum foil and bake in a preheated 300 degree F. oven for 1 hour.

You could hurry this up by baking at 350 degrees F. for about a half hour. I prefer to bake it slowly so it doesn't bubble over and has more 'time for flavors to mingle.

Sprinkle each roll with a tablespoon (or less) of sapsago cheese before serving.

• BAKED VEGETABLES •

BROCCOLI MUSHROOM BAKE

Yield: 1 serving

1 medium-size onion, chopped
1/2 cup low-fat cottage cheese
2 tablespoons skim milk
3 dashes Tabasco sauce
1 cup chopped broccoli florets
4 large mushrooms, sliced
2 slices Pritikin or commercial whole wheat bread
1/2 cup Brown Turkey Gravy (page 231) or chicken gravy (from
*   Country Chicken Stew, page 116)*

Put one quarter of the onion in a blender along with 1/4 cup of the cottage cheese, the skim milk, and the Tabasco sauce. Blend until smooth. Set aside.

Combine the broccoli, mushrooms, and remaining onions, in a nonstick pan, and sauté until the broccoli begins to get tender.

Meanwhile, toast the bread lightly and place on an ovenproof dinner plate. Cover the toast with the sautéed broccoli mixture. Spoon the remaining 1/4 cup cottage cheese on top. Place the plate on the top shelf of the oven and bake for 10 minutes at 400 degrees F. Heat the gravy and pour over the broccoli and cottage cheese. Over the gravy, pour the blended cottage cheese and onion.

ZUCCHINI SOUR CREAM BAKE

Yield: 1 serving

2 slices Pritikin or commercial whole wheat bread
1 medium-size zucchini
1/4 cup low-fat cottage cheese
3/4 cup chicken gravy (from Country Chicken Stew, page 116)
*   or Brown Turkey Gravy (page 231)*
1/4 cup Mock Sour Cream (page 215)

Place the bread slices next to each other on a ovenproof dinner plate. Slice the zucchini thinly and arrange on top of the bread.

Microwave Directions

Cook for 1 minute on high.

Oven Directions

Bake in a preheated 350 degree F. oven for 5-6 minutes.

Remove from the microwave or oven and spread the cottage cheese on top of the zucchini. Bake on the top shelf of a preheated 350 degree F. oven for about 10 minutes. Heat the gravy and pour over the melted cottage cheese. Top with Mock Sour Cream.

ACORN SQUASH CHEESE BAKE

• • • • • • • • • • • • • • • • • • • •

Yield: 2 servings

1 medium-size whole acorn squash
1/2 cup low-fat cottage cheese
1 tablespoon finely chopped onion
1/2 medium-size apple, peeled and chopped
1/4 cup raisins
1 tablespoon apple juice concentrate
1 tablespoon grated sapsago cheese

Microwave Directions

Prick squash with a fork and set on a plate. Microwave on high 8 minutes. Cool and divide in half the long way. Remove seeds.

Stove Top Directions

Boil squash in water to cover until tender, 15-20 minutes after water starts to boil. Cool and divide in half the long way. Remove seeds.

Mix together the cottage cheese, onion, apple, and raisins.

Pour about 1-1/2 teaspoons of the juice concentrate in the cavity of each squash and "woosh" it around to coat the insides of the squash with the juice. Fill the cavities with the cottage cheese mixture. Let sit in the refrigerator, covered with plastic wrap, for at least 15-30 minutes to plump up the raisins and let the different tastes mingle.

Sprinkle with sapsago cheese and bake for 15 minutes in a 325 degree F. oven. Serve hot.

STUFFED EGGPLANT

• • • • • • • • • • • • • • • • • • • •

Yield: 2 servings

1 large eggplant
1 large onion, chopped
1 small green pepper
4 garlic cloves, finely chopped
3 slices Pritikin or whole wheat bread, crumbed
1/3 cup rose wine
2/3 cup low-fat cottage cheese
1 teaspoon powdered or crumbled thyme
1/4 teaspoon ground bay leaf
2 egg whites
1/4 cup chopped fresh parsley
Cayenne pepper
4 teaspoons grated sapsago cheese

Microwave Directions

Cut the eggplant in half the long way and place on a dish. Microwave on high for 12 minutes. Let the eggplant cool.

Stove Top Directions

In a large pot, cover the whole eggplant with water. Boil for 25-30 minutes, until tender. Test with a sharp knife for tenderness, but be careful not to tear the skin too much. Remove the eggplant from the pot very carefully and place on a chopping board. Let it cool. Cut in half the long way.

Place the 2 halves cut side up on a nonstick baking pan. Scoop out the pulp and put it in a bowl. Cutting around the edges of the pulp with a very sharp knife helps to loosen it. Set the halves and pulp aside.

Combine the onion and green pepper in a nonstick frying pan. Turn the heat on high and sauté until lightly browned. Add the eggplant. Add the remaining ingredients, except the sapsago cheese, and mix thoroughly. Pile into eggplant shells, sprinkle with cheese. Bake at 350 degrees F. for 20-25 minutes.

Variations

Shrimp-Stuffed Eggplant. Weigh the shrimp after you peel them

---

for exact portions. Figure that 8-10 peeled shrimp will equal two 1-1/2 ounce servings. Add the shrimp to the stuffing instead of the cottage cheese.

Rice and Chili-Stuffed Eggplant. Substitute 1 cup cooked brown rice (page 233) for bread crumbs. Omit the wine and add 1-1/2 peeled and chopped green chilies. Use whole ones and chop them (the whole ones have more flavor than the ones that come chopped). Rinse the canned chilies if you are very, very stict about your sodium intake, otherwise, leave them as is. Also, add 2 teaspoons of red hot sauce (not Tabasco).

After you sauté the vegetables, add 1 cup water and the eggplant and mash around with back of your spoon. Add the seasonings and egg whites. Reduce the heat to medium and let the water cook out, stirring all the while. Then add the rice and cottage cheese. Stuff the eggplant shells and bake as directed above.

STUFFED IRISH POTATO
• • • • • • • • • • • • • • • • • • • •
Yield: 1 serving

1 medium-size Irish potato
1/2 cup Mock Sour Cream (page 215)
1 green onion, sliced in rings (optional)

Microwave Directions
Prick the potato with a fork and bake in the microwave on high for 6-7 minutes. Horizontally split open the cooked potato with a knife and push the ends in to crumble the contents. Scoop out the potato and place the contents in a small bowl. Mix in the Mock Sour Cream. Return the mixture to the potato shell and bake for 2 minutes on high.

Oven Directions
Bake the potato at 350 degrees F. for 45-60 minutes. Pierce with a sharp knife to see if it is done. Horizontally split open the cooked potato with a knife and push the ends in to crumble the contents. Scoop out the potato and place the contents in a small bowl. Mix in the Mock Sour Cream. Return the mixture to the potato shell and bake in a preheated 350 degree F. oven for 15-20 minutes until heated through. Garnish with onion rings if you wish.

SCALLOPED POTATOES

· ·

Yield: 3-4 servings

2 large Irish potatoes or 5 little ones (enough to equal
2-1/2 cups sliced)
1/2 cup chopped green onions and tops (or white onion)
2 cups skim milk
3 tablespoons whole wheat flour
1 teaspoon dried basil
3-4 sprinkles cayenne pepper
Paprika (optional)

Bake or boil the potatoes in their peels until tender. Cool and peel. Slice into a 1-1/2-quart baking dish. Mix in the green onions.

In a blender, mix together the milk, flour, basil, and cayenne. Pour over the potatoes.

Microwave Directions

Microwave, uncovered, on bake at 60 percent power for 20 minutes.

Oven Directions

Bake, uncovered at 350 degrees F. for about 30 minutes, until the sauce is thickened.

When done, stir the top a little to blend in a foam that forms. Sprinkle with a little paprika for color, if desired. Serve warm.

· SPAGHETTI PLUS ·

SPAGHETTI WITH ONIONS AND ZUCCHINI FOR ONE

· · · · · · · · · · · · · · · · · · · ·

Yield: 1 serving

6 ounces whole wheat spaghetti
1/2-3/4 cup Roast Beef Gravy I (page 228) or II (page 230)
1 large onion, coarsely chopped
1 medium-size zucchini, cubed
1/16 teaspoon cayenne pepper
1/4 cup low-fat cottage cheese

Weigh the raw spaghetti. If you don't have a scale get a tape measure. Grab a big handful and holding the spaghetti together, measure. Aim for a handful that measures 3-1/2 inches around.

Put a pot of water on to boil for the spaghetti, and heat the gravy in a small pan. When the water starts to boil, add the spaghetti and give it stir. After about 5 minutes, stir again. Cook for about 15 minutes. Whole wheat spaghetti takes longer to cook than semolina spaghetti. If it is undercooked, it tastes grainy. When the spaghetti is done, drain it.

In the meantime, chop the vegetables and combine them in a nonstick frying pan. Turn the heat on high, sauté the vegetables, and sprinkle with the cayenne while sautéing. Continue to sauté until the vegetables are cooked through but still a little bit crunchy. Taste. The onions should be fairly limp and somewhat transparent. Remove from the heat.

With everything cooked and hot, place the drained spaghetti on a large plate. Pile the onions and zucchini on top. On top of the vegetables, spread the cottage cheese. No need to heat the cheese. On top of cheese, pour the gravy. Serve immediately.

CREAMED SPAGHETTI MILANO
• • • • • • • • • • • • • • • • • • •
Yield: 2-4 servings

This tastes very much like Fettuccine Alfredo.

2/3 cup skim milk
1/4 teaspoon red pepper flakes
1/2 teaspoon dried parsley flakes or 1 tablespoon fresh chopped
1/2 teaspoon dried oregano
1/4 teaspoon garlic powder
1/2 teaspoon onion powder
1 tablespoon cornstarch
2 cups cooked spaghetti (use whole wheat if you like)
Grated sapsago cheese

Pour the milk into a small saucepan. Add the seasonings and cornstarch and stir until well mixed. Place the saucepan over medium heat and stir until the mixture bubbles. Remove from heat, and add the hot, cooked spaghetti and mix well with the sauce. Sprinkle a tablespoon of grated sapsago cheese over each serving.

TREE EARS AND NOODLES

• • • • • • • • • • • • • • • • • •

Yield: 2 servings

Tree ears are something like regular white mushrooms but the texture is definitely different and more interesting. They can be found in oriental stores, as well as gourmet stores, where they also go by the names of cloud ears, wood ears, black fungus, tree fungus, or Szechuan mushrooms.

1/4 cup dry tree ears (or 2 cups sliced fresh mushrooms)
1/2 cup hot water
3/4 cup fresh or frozen snow pea pods
1 large onion, coarsely chopped
1/2 large green pepper, coarsely chopped
1 large carrot, finely chopped
1 large yellow squash, finely chopped
1 teaspoon low-sodium tamari or soy sauce
1 tablespoon plus 1 teaspoon rose wine
1 (6-1/2-ounce) can water chestnuts, drained and sliced
1/2 cup low-fat cottage cheese
1 cup cooked imitation egg noodles (or substitute cooked whole wheat
  spaghetti)
1/2 cup chicken gravy (from Country Chicken Stew, page 116) or
  Brown Turkey Gravy (page 231)

First, soak the tree ears in hot water. By the time you have finished chopping the other vegetables in the recipe, they should be soft. They take about 20 minutes to open up into "flowers." Drain the tree ears and feel them to see if they have any tough knots. Remove any knots and chop the rest into pieces about the size of any sliced mushroom.

Put the snow peas, onion, green pepper, carrot, squash, and tamari or soy sauce in a nonstick frying pan. Add the fresh mushrooms now if you do not use tree ears. Turn the heat on high and saute' until the onion looks transparent and a little brown. Add the wine and sauté for about 30 seconds. Add the tree ears, water chestnuts, cottage cheese, noodles, and gravy. Mix all together and taste to see if it is hot enough. If not, cover and heat through for about 1 minute. Serve with Chinese Mustard Sauce (page 226).

NOODLES VILLA D'ESTE

Yield: 6-8 servings

The Roman Emperor Hadrian's magnificent palace, Villa d'Este, about 20 miles northwest of Rome, was built around 100 A.D. It is still perfectly preserved. My husband and I sat in a little café overlooking the Italian countryside, and in the shadow of the Villa, ate something very similar to this.

1-1/2 cups uncooked whole wheat elbow macaroni
Italian Tomato Sauce (page 232)
1-1/2 cups low-fat cottage cheese
1 (10-ounce) package chopped spinach, defrosted
1 large zucchini, sliced Sapsago cheese

Cook the macaroni in plenty of boiling water for 16 minutes, or until done. Drain.

In a 9-inch by 13-inch baking dish, layer the tomato sauce, half the macaroni, half the cottage cheese and all of the spinach. Top with the remaining cooked macaroni, more tomato sauce, the remaining cottage cheese, and the raw sliced zucchini. Finish up with tomato sauce. Bake at 350 degrees F. for 40 minutes. Serve with a sprinkle of grated sapsago cheese on top.

This can be refrigerated, cut into squares about 4 inches wide, placed in plastic bags, and frozen for several other meals.

FUNNY PIZZA

• • • • • • • • • • • • • • • • • • •

Yield: 1 serving

1 slice Pritikin or commercial whole wheat bread
1 large mushroom, sliced
1/2 small onion, minced
1/4 cup Italian Tomato Sauce (page 232)
1/4 cup low-fat cottage cheese
1 tablespoon grated sapsago cheese

Put the bread on an ovenproof plate and spread the tomato sauce on top. Use a little extra sauce if you want. Arrange the mushroom slices, then the minced onion, on top. Bake in a preheated 350 degree F. oven for about 10 minutes, or until mushrooms are limp and the bread begins to look toasted.

Remove from the oven, spread the cottage cheese, and sprinkle the sapsago cheese on top. Return to the oven for 5 minutes to heat the cheeses through. Serve.

For variety, use zucchini and green pepper slices, as well as the mushrooms and onions.

❊ TURKEY STUFFING

• • • • • • • • • • • • • • • • • • •

Yield: 2-4 servings

6 slices of Pritikin or commercial whole wheat bread
1 large onion, chopped
3 celery ribs, chopped
1 large green pepper, chopped
2 cups turkey or chicken stock
1/2 cup chopped fresh parsley
1 teaspoon powdered or crumbled thyme
1 teaspoon dried sage
1 teaspoon dried marjoram
1 teaspoon garlic powder
Red pepper flakes to taste

Process the bread into crumbs in a food processor. Set aside. Place the onion, celery, and green pepper in a nonstick frying pan and turn the heat on high. Sauté by turning the vegetables over and over

---

until the onion looks a little brown around the edges and somewhat transparent. Add the turkey or chicken stock. Cover and cook on medium heat for 5-6 minutes, until the vegetables are tender. Add the bread crumbs, parsley, and seasonings. Mix well. Taste for more seasoning. Place in an 8-inch by 8-inch nonstick pan. Bake at 350 degrees F. for 20 minutes.

Spoon Brown Turkey Gravy (page 231) over the stuffing and serve with Cranberry Sauce (page 224).

Variation

Oyster Stuffing. Buy a dozen fresh oysters in a jar of liquid. Measure the liquid and add enough turkey or chicken stock to make 2 cups. Add the liiquid and the oysters to the stuffing just before baking. You can also use any size can of unsmoked oysters. Weigh the drained oysters for the exact meat serving size.

• MEATLESS RICE DISHES •
ORIENTAL "FRIED" RICE

Yield: 2 servings

1 large onion, coarsely chopped
1 (10-ounce) package frozen or 1-1/2 cups fresh snow pea pods
1/2 teaspoon low-sodium tamari or soy sauce
2 egg whites
2/3 cup cooked brown rice (page 233)
1/4 teaspoon cayenne pepper or more to taste

Combine the onion, snow peas, and tamari or soy sauce in a nonstick frying pan. Turn the heat on high and sauté. When the onion begins to look brown around the edges and fairly limp and transparent, add the egg whites and rice. Stir. Reduce the heat to low and cover. Cook for 4 minutes, or until the eggs are cooked and the snow peas are tender. Stir in the cayenne and serve. Chinese Mustard Sauce (page 226) and/or Sweet and Sour Sauce (page 227) go well with this dish.

For variety you can add browned, drained lean ground beef, cooked chicken, or even low fat cottage cheese. Raw shrimp or raw chicken pieces can be sautéed with the vegetables.

MEXICORN AND RICE

Yield: 5-6 six servings

2 cups frozen chuck wagon style corn (or any frozen corn that
*   contains whole kernel corn, green and red bell peppers,*
*   and onions)*
1 cup cooked brown rice and wild rice, or cooked
*   brown rice (page 233)*
1 jalapeno, sliced (or less)
1/4 teaspoon garlic powder
1 teaspoon onion powder
3-6 tablespoons water

Microwave Directions

Mix the corn, rice, jalapeno, and seasonings in a 1-quart container. Add 3 tablespoons water. Cover and cook on high for 3 minutes. Stir. Cook, covered, for 3 more minutes. Serve immediately.

Stove Top Directions

Combine the corn, rice, jalapeno, and seasonings in a bowl. Bring 6 tablespoons of water to a boil in a saucepan. Add the corn mixture and cover. Turn the heat to medium and cook for 3-4 minutes, until the corn is tender. Serve immediately.

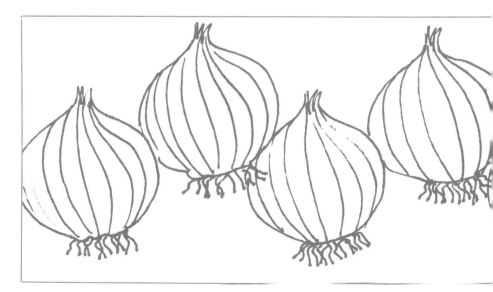

✳ BROCCOLI PILAF

Yield: 4-5 servings

This is a good recipe to make if you have some leftover cooked rice.

*1-1/2 cups cooked brown and wild rice or cooked brown
    rice (page 233)*
2 cups cooked chopped broccoli
2 egg whites
1/4 teaspoon cayenne pepper
1 tablespoon dried onion flakes or 1 medium-size onion, chopped
5-6 tomato slices
2-1/2 tablespoons sapsago cheese

Mix together the rice, broccoli, egg whites, cayenne, and onion in a 1-quart baking dish. Place the tomato slices over the top. Sprinkle with the sapsago cheese and bake, uncovered, at 300 degrees F. for 40 minutes. Serve at once.

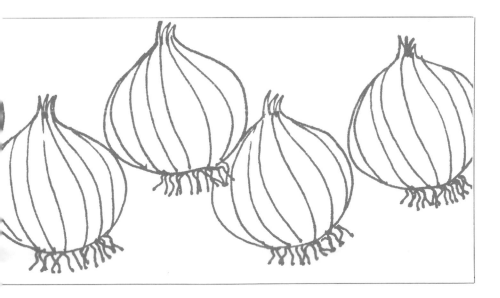

HAWAIIAN RICE *TERRIBLE!*

Yield: 7-8 servings

Do try to get some wild rice to mix in as it really tastes much better than the brown rice alone. With its sweet, tropical, nutlike quality, this tastes good served along with Oven-Fried Chicken and Cranberry Baked Squash. Leftovers will freeze well.

1-1/4 cups uncooked long-grain brown rice and wild rice (or just brown rice)
1/2 cup drained crushed unsweetened pineapple (reserve the juice)
1/2 cup raisins
1/2 large apple, peeled and cubed
1 small onion, coarsely chopped
1 (8-ounce) can water chestnuts, sliced
1 celery rib, chopped
1/4 teaspoon red pepper flakes
1 tablespoon apple juice concentrate
1/4 teaspoon turmeric
Juice drained from pineapple plus enough water to equal 2-1/2 cups
2 tablespoons low-sodium tamari or soy sauce

Place all the ingredients in a 1-1/2-quart casserole dish. Stir with a fork.

Microwave Directions

Cover the baking dish and microwave on simmer or 50 percent power for 55 minutes. Let sit, covered, for 15-20 minutes, fluff and mix with a fork, and serve.

Oven Directions

Bake, covered, on the middle rack of a preheated 300 degree F. oven for 55 minutes. Let sit, covered, for 15-20 minutes, fluff and mix with a fork, and serve.

✳ SPANISH RICE

• • • • • • • • • • • • • • • • • • •

Yield: 6 servings

Spanish Rice is especially good served with black beans or pinto beans.

1 cup chopped onion
1 cup chopped green pepper
1 tablespoon chopped fresh parsley, firmly packed
2 cups water
1 small tomato, chopped
4 teaspoons chili powder
1/8-1/4 teaspoon red pepper flakes
1/2 teaspoon garlic powder
1 tablespoon no-salt tomato paste
1 cup uncooked brown and wild rice or brown rice

Combine the onion, pepper, and parsley in a nonstick frying pan. Turn the heat on high and sauté until the onion looks brown around the edges and a little transparent. Add the water. Stir. Add the tomato, chili powder, red pepper flakes, garlic powder, and tomato paste. Remove from the heat. Pour the rice into a 1-1/2-quart casserole dish. Add all the other ingredients. Stir and cover.

Microwave Directions

Microwave on simmer or 50 percent power for 55 minutes. Let stand, covered, for 15-20 minutes. Mix and fluff with a fork.

Oven Directions

Bake in a preheated 300 degree F. oven for 55 minutes. Let stand, covered, for 15-20 minutes. Mix and fluff with a fork.

For variety, substitute 1 (3-1/2-ounce) can of whole green chili peppers, chopped, for the green pepper.

CHAPTER 6

MAIN DISHES WITH MEAT AND FISH

HERE ARE MENUS THAT WILL SOUND MORE FAMILIAR TO YOU.

Once you have lowered your blood cholesterol levels on a regression diet, it is legal to have a little meat: about 3-1/2 ounces of beef, chicken or fish every day. It is better to plan more meals with fish or chicken during a week that it is to plan ones with red meat since the fish and chicken contain fewer calories and less fat and cholesterol.

Menus containing meat are for a maintenance or a normal diet. You won't lose weight with this, but you can maintain a normal weight.

An average man over forty, maintaining a normal weight, can eat 2,000 calories a day. The menus that follow contain about 1,000 calories or less, leaving you 500 calories or more for each lunch and breakfast. A woman should reduce the amounts slightly. To tell you the truth, I can't even eat as much in one sitting as I have here in each menu, so I spread some of this out or I don't eat 500 calories for breakfast or lunch. But, then I'm not such a big eater. These menus were planned considering what I know my husband can eat; he is a tremendous eater — a virtual bottomless pit. I'm sure there are a lot of other bottomless pits out there too.

MEAL NO. 1

Start with a bowl of Black Bean Potato Soup, then serve a plate with one sixth of a Chicken Quiche, 1/2 cup Indian Corn With Peppers, and 1 cup of mixed steamed zucchini and yellow squash. Serve a small portion of colorful Peter Rabbit Salad. For dessert, one quarter of a recipe for Banana Raisin Pudding in a pretty dish. About 930 calories in all.

MEAL NO. 2

This meal contains only about 803 calories. Start with 1 cup of Beaucoup Bean Soup. Follow with Socrates Salad, a Gyro Sandwich with a 2-ounce serving of meat topped with 1/4 cup of Imitation Mayonnaise along with 1 cup of steamed spinach. Turn down the lights and end up this satisfying meal with Crepes Patrician and flaming brandy over the top.

MEAL NO. 3

Try Mushroom Soup, 3 ounces of Oven-Fried Catfish, 1 cup of steamed cauliflower, a Stuffed Sweet Potato, a simple lettuce and tomato salad with Italian Salad Dressing, and one sixth of a Cheesecake for a delicious meal that is just about 1,000 calories.

MEAL NO. 4

For something fancy and delicious serve some Black Bean Celery Soup, Coquille San Jacques, 1 cup of steamed spinach, one quarter of a recipe for Carrot Salad Supreme, and one sixth of a Blueberry Cream Pie for dessert. About 971 calories.

MEAL NO. 5

How is this for a normal sounding meal at about 900 calories? Begin with 1 cup of French Onion Soup and one quarter of a recipe for Mardi Gras Salad. Follow this with 1-1/2 ounces of lean roast beef, 1 cup of Cheesy Mashed Potatoes topped with delicious Roast Beef Gravy I or II, and 1 cup of mixed steamed peas and carrots. Serve Lemon Cream Pie for dessert.

MEAL NO. 6

This meal with only about 703 calories has a Mexican flair. Begin with one fifth of a recipe for French Potato Leek Soup. Then serve 2 tacos with low-fat cottage cheese on top, Senorita Salad, and 1 cup of steamed brussels sprouts. For dessert: a Baked Apple With Raisins.

MEAL NO. 7

One of my favorite meals at about 860 calories is 1 cup of Split Pea Soup, 2 cups of Stewed Eggplant over 2/3 cup of brown rice, a 3-ounce piece of lean broiled steak, 1/2 cup serving of Cole Slaw a la Tropique, and Blackberry Pie for dessert.

MEAL NO. 8

For a meal with a soul food taste, try 1 cup of Blueberry Soup, 2 cups of Jambalaya au Congri, 1/2 cup of mixed steamed broccoli and cauliflower, 1 cup of Collards and Carrots, 1 slice of commercial or 2 slices of homemade whole wheat bread spread thickly with 1/4 cup of Creole Cream Cheese, 2 mock stuffed eggs, a simple lettuce and tomato salad with B & B Dressing, and Strawberry Cream Dessert for dessert. That's just about 1,000 calories.

MEAL NO. 9

A festive meal of under 800 calories is Poulet Sauce Cerise (Chicken with Cherry Sauce), using a 3-ounce chicken breast and 1 cup of the Cherry Glaze. Begin the meal with 1 cup of Hearty Squash Soup and serve with 1/2 recipe of Creamed Spaghetti Milano, 1 cup of steamed spinach, 1/2 cup of steamed carrots, a simple lettuce, cucumber, and tomato salad with Italian Salad Dressing, and a slice of Holiday Fruitcake for dessert.

MEAL NO. 10

For a bright delicious start, begin with Strawberry Mountain and a cup of Broccoli Chowder. Then go on to a Stuffed Green Pepper which is cooked Creole style. Add 2 cups of Red Cabbage and Carrots. Have one sixth of a recipe for Tutti Fruiti Treat for dessert. This runs about 902 calories.

MEAL NO. 11

One cup of New Orleans Style Seafood Gumbo served over 1/2 cup of brown rice makes a very rich meal. Three toasted French Rolls or 2 slices of toasted Oat Bran Bread for dunking would be really satisfying. Add to that 1 serving of Full Meal Salad topped with 1/2 cup B & B Dressing. Have one sixth of a Cheesecake for dessert for a meal of about 821 calories.

MEAL NO. 12

Three ounces of Baked Trout is delicious with one quarter of a recipe for Creamy Baked Onions, a large boiled potato cut in a few pieces, 1 cup of mixed green peas and sliced carrots and 1 cup of steamed cauliflower. Start the meal with a cup of Split Pea Soup and a simple lettuce and tomato salad with Greek Dressing. A wonderfully refreshing dessert would be a generous serving of Fresh Fruit Firenze. This is about 930 calories.

MEAL NO. 13

A really elegant meal begins with Old-Fashioned Salad. One third of a recipe for Oyster Soup, 3 French rolls for dunking, 2 steamed spears of broccoli on the side and one sixth of a Blueberry Cream Pie for dessert adds up to about 875 calories.

Knowing how to make a plate look attractive is most important to the enjoyment of food. See page 85 for some hints.

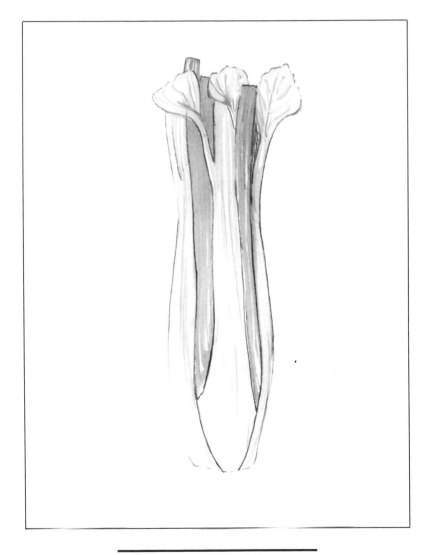

• CHICKEN AND FOWL •

CHICKEN QUICHE

Yield: 4-6 servings

Crust

1 cup Grape-nuts
1/2 cup skim milk

Pour the Grape-nuts into a 9-inch pie pan and mix with the milk. Press the mixture with the back of a spoon to the shape of the pie shell.

Filling

1 cup diced chicken meat (cooked or uncooked)
1 medium-size onion, coarsely chopped
1 medium-size green pepper, coarsely chopped
3 mushrooms, sliced (optional)
6 egg whites
1 cup skim milk
3 tablespoons whole wheat flour
1/16 teaspoon cayenne pepper or more to taste
1/2 teaspoon sage
Paprika

Distribute the chicken and vegetables over the crust.

In a food processor or blender, combine the egg whites, milk, flour, cayenne, and sage. Blend or process until thoroughly mixed. Pour over the chicken mixture. Bake in a preheated 350 degree F. oven for 40-45 minutes. Let cool for 10 minutes before cutting. Sprinkle with a little paprika for extra color.

This can be frozen in pieces and saved for a meal when you have had a busy day. Just reheat the frozen pieces of quiche covered with plastic wrap on medium power in the microwave for 5-10 minutes. Or cover with aluminum foil and reheat in a oven at 300 degrees F. for about 20 minutes.

If the quiche is divided in 6 slices, each slice will contain 1 ounce of chicken. Divided into 4, each slice will contain about 2 ounces of chicken, and that will be a very large slice of quiche.

COUNTRY CHICKEN STEW

Yield: 6-8 servings

My mother used to make the best chicken stew. I can still remember today how it smelled simmering in her kitchen. That tender, juicy chicken and rich gravy over rice was just wonderful. I use many of her techniques and ingredients plus some of my own in cooking this stew. It tastes almost identical. Extra gravy can be saved and used in other dishes such as Zucchini Sour Cream Bake.

8 chicken pieces (breasts, legs, or a whole chicken, cut up)
1/4 teaspoon cayenne pepper
2 medium-size to large onions, chopped
1 medium-size to large green pepper, chopped
4 garlic cloves, chopped
6 tablespoons whole wheat flour
Water or chicken stock
1 teaspoon powdered or crumbled thyme
2 bay leaves
1/8 teaspoon turmeric
1/2 teaspoon sage
1/4 cup dry vermouth
1-1/2 teaspoons red hot sauce (not Tabasco)
1 tablespoon dried or 1/4 cup chopped fresh parsley, loosely packed
1/4 cup apple juice concentrate

Skin the chicken pieces. Remove as much fat as possible. Place as many pieces of chicken as you can in a single layer in a large nonstick pot. Do not stack the pieces on top of each other. Turn the heat on high. Sprinkle a little cayenne on top. Brown the chicken on both sides, moving them around every now and then. Remove the pieces from the pot when brown.

The pot may be smoking by this time; if it is, reduce the heat to medium and quickly add more chicken to the pot. Brown as you did the first pieces. Increase the heat if the chicken seems to be browning very slowly, looking more like it is steaming than browning; do not let the pot smoke. Continue in this manner until all the chicken has browned. Remove the chicken and set aside.

Pour off any grease that accumulated in the pot, and wipe the pot with a paper towel, but do not wipe clean the caramelized juices.

Return the pot to stove and add the onions, green pepper, and garlic. Turn the heat to high. Sauté until fairly brown. If the vegetables start smoking, reduce the heat a little. Sprinkle the flour over the vegetables and continue to sauté, turning the vegetables over and over. The flour will start to smoke. Continue saute'ing for about 20 seconds more, stirring constantly. Immediately add 2 cups of the water or stock, a little at a time, while you continue to stir. Continue to stir until smooth. Reduce the heat to low. Add the remaining ingredients.

Return the chicken to the pot, and add more water or stock if needed to cover the chicken. Simmer, covered, for 1-1/2-2 hours. Stir occasionally and add a little more water if the gravy cooks down to more than 1/4 inch below the chicken pieces. The gravy should be a little thicker than melted ice cream.

Cool in the refrigerator overnight. The next day, remove any grease that has hardened on the top. Reheat and serve the chicken and gravy over brown rice. Save and freeze extra gravy in small containers for future meals.

One breast or one thigh and drumstick weighs 3-1/2-4 ounces. Bone the meat and weigh for exact measures.

VARIATION

Chicken and Dumplings. Mix 1/2 cup whole wheat flour and 1/2 teaspoon low-sodium baking powder. Mix in 1 egg white and 6 tablespoons skim milk. Drop by the teaspoonful into the just simmering chicken stew gravy. Poach for about 10 minutes or until little air bubbles or holes appear on top of each dumpling. When you see the air holes that means they are just about done. Let them cook a wee bit longer to make sure they are cooked through. Serve at once with the stew, brown rice and gravy.

These are not round like a ball dumplings. They turn out more the shape of little inflated pancakes. If you try to add more flour so you can roll them into a ball like conventional dumplings, they will be tough.

CHICKEN CREPES

Yield: 2 servings

1 medium-size onion, chopped
1 small to medium-size green pepper, chopped
2 cups water
1 carrot, chopped
4 ounces lean cooked chicken breast, diced
1/8 teaspoon cayenne pepper
1/4 teaspoon garlic powder
1-1/2 teaspoons orange juice concentrate
4-1/2 teaspoons apple juice concentrate
1/2 teaspoon dried parsley flakes
1/4 teaspoon powdered or crumbled thyme
1 teaspoon low-sodium soy or tamari sauce
2 tablespoons unbleached white flour
2 crepes (page 221)

Combine the onion and green pepper in a nonstick 1-1/2 quart saucepan. Turn the heat on high and sauté for 3-4 minutes, until the onion is tender. Add the water, carrot, chicken, cayenne, garlic, orange and apple juice concentrates, parsley, thyme, and tamari or soy sauce. Bring to a boil and boil fast, uncovered, to reduce the mixture by about half. This will take about 8 minutes.

Strain the liquid from the vegetables into a measuring cup. You want to have 1 cup of liquid. Add enough water to make 1 cup, if necessary. Return the liquid to the vegetables and bring to a boil again. Add the flour by sprinkling 1 teaspoon at a time over the boiling mixture and mixing it in well. Keep adding flour until it is all mixed in. Boil for about 30 seconds or until the mixture thickens, stirring constantly. It will not be extremely thick. It just makes a nice gravy.

Keep warm while you prepare the crepes.

Pour the filling on 2 open crepes on 2 plates. Then fold the crepes in half and pour more sauce on top. Serve.

Each person will get a 2-ounce serving of chicken. For the regression diet, use only 3 ounces of chicken for this recipe, so each gets 1-1/2 ounces of meat.

LITTLE CHICKEN NUGGETS

• • • • • • • • • • • • • • • • • • •

Yield: 2 servings

1 chicken breast, boned and skinned
Turmeric
Basil
Cayenne pepper
Sage
1 egg white
1 tablespoon plus 2 teaspoons oat bran or whole wheat flour

It will be easier to slice the chicken if it is partially frozen. Slice the chicken to make pieces 1/4 inch wide.

Add a sprinkle of all the spices to the raw egg white and beat. Dip each piece of chicken in the egg white and then into the oat bran or flour to coat. Place on a nonstick pan and bake for 15-20 minutes at 350 degrees F. When the bottoms brown, turn over and brown the other side. They will not get extremely brown to be done.

Serve with a dinner of vegetables and at least one complex carbohydrate, such as potatoes or beans. Dip the little nuggets into no-salt Dijon mustard, which can be purchased at a gourmet store, or Sweet and Sour Sauce and Chinese Mustard Sauce.

OVEN-FRIED CHICKEN

• • • • • • • • • • • • • • • • • • • •

Yield: 4-5 servings

If you get a yen for some good old fried chicken, try this. It is not greasy, but it definitely has that fried chicken taste.

8-10 chicken pieces or a whole chicken, cut up
1/2 cup skim milk
1 egg white
1/4 teaspoon sage
1/2 teaspoon onion powder
1/4 teaspoon powdered or crumbled thyme
3-4 drops Tabasco sauce
1-1/2 cups whole wheat flour
1/4 teaspoon cayenne pepper

Skin the chicken pieces, removing every little bit of fat.

Mix together the milk, egg white, sage, onion powder, thyme, and Tabasco sauce.

Put the flour in a plastic bag with the cayenne and shake.

Dip each piece of chicken in the milk mixture and shake one at a time in the flour until coated. Place on a nonstick baking sheet or pan.

Take a piece of aluminum foil about 2 feet by 1 foot and wad it up to make a roll about a foot long. Place it at the back of the rack in the oven to form a "pillow." Place the pan in the oven with the "pillow" under one end. If there is any fat or grease left in the chicken, it will roll toward the opposite end from the "pillow" and the chicken won't sit in grease. Bake in a preheated 350 degree F. oven for about 30 minutes, or until tender and cooked through. Turn once.

One chicken breast or one thigh and drumstick together is equal to 3-1/2-4 ounces of meat.

If you are on a very strict diet, you might want to skin and bone half a breast, cut it in half again and weigh it. The meat will come to about 1-1/2 ounces. Trim off meat until you have exactly 1-1/2 ounces, then flour and bake the chicken as above.

BAKED CHICKEN

. . . .

Yield: 4-5 servings

Some people like a little fresh lemon juice squeezed over this chicken. See what you like. My kids love chicken this way. They don't even notice there is no salt.

1 whole 3-1/2-pound chicken
Cayenne pepper
Garlic powder
Onion powder

Remove the skin from chicken and trim off as much of the fat remaining as you can. Sprinkle lightly with the cayenne, garlic powder, and onion powder.

Microwave Directions

Bake, uncovered, at 80 percent power or on roast for 30-40 minutes. With a very sharp knife, pierce the chicken in the very meaty part of the thigh near where it is connected to the back. If any red juice comes out, cook the chicken for 5-6 minutes longer.

Oven Directions

Bake for 1 hour at 350 degrees F. with an aluminum foil tent over the chicken. When the legs are loose and easy to lift up and down, the chicken is done. Just to make sure, pierce in the meaty part of the thigh near where it is connected to the back. If any red or pink juice runs out, bake the chicken a little longer.

One breast or one thigh and drumstick is equal to 3-1/2-4 ounces of meat.

CHICKEN TROPICANA

● ● ● ● ● ● ● ● ● ● ● ● ● ● ● ● ● ● ● ●

Yield: 4-5 servings

This dish is great with Cabbage Extravaganza. A little Chinese Mustard Sauce served on the side really gives this dish extra zing.

3-1/2-pound chicken, skinned and cut up
1/4 plus 1/16 teaspoon cayenne pepper
1/4 teaspoon curry powder
2-1/2 cups unsweetened pineapple juice
1/4 cup plus 2 tablespoons apple juice concentrate
1/3 cup brandy, whiskey, or rum
1 large onion, chopped
1/3 cup raisins
1 cup drained unsweetened crushed pineapple, fresh or canned
1/4 teaspoon dried basil
1 tablespoon arrowroot or cornstarch

I like to skin my chicken whole, starting at the bottom of the breast. I just keep cutting underneath and pulling. Then I cut up the chicken, and remove any skin that is left, as well as any pockets of fat.

Microwave Directions

Place the chicken pieces in a 9-inch by 13-inch baking dish. Sprinkle the chicken with 1/8 teaspoon of the cayenne and 1/8 teaspoon of the curry powder. Bake on high for 15 minutes to brown the chicken.

Remove from the microwave and turn the chicken over. Pour in 1-1/2 cups of the pineapple juice, 1/4 cup of the juice concentrate, and the brandy, whiskey, or rum. Stir in the onion, raisins, and pineapple. Sprinkle on 1/16 teaspoon of the cayenne and the basil.

Bake for 15 minutes on high, basting occasionally. Then simmer for 15 minutes.

Remove the chicken from the pan and keep warm. Sprinkle the arrowroot or cornstarch into the pan and work it into the liquid with the back of your spoon, then stir it into the pan juices until smooth. Add the remaining 1 cup pineapple juice, 2 tablespoons juice concentrate, 1/8 teaspoon cayenne, and 1/8 teaspoon curry powder.

Bake on high for 7 minutes, stirring often. If the mixture doesn't thicken, stir in a little more arrowroot or cornstarch. If it becomes too thick, add more pineapple juice and a little more juice concentrate.

Oven Directions

Place the chicken pieces in a 9-inch by 13-inch baking dish. Sprinkle the chicken with 1/8 teaspoon of the cayenne and 1/8 teaspoon of the curry powder. Cover loosely with aluminum foil, leaving air vents on the side. Bake in a preheated 400 degree F. oven for 20-25 minutes to brown the chicken.

Remove from the oven and turn the chicken over. Pour in 1-1/2 cups of the pineapple juice, 1/4 cup of the juice concentrate and the brandy, whiskey, or rum. Stir in the onion, raisins, and pineapple. Sprinkle on 1/16 teaspoon cayenne and 1/4 teaspoon basil. Lower the oven temperature to 250 degrees F. and bake, loosely covered with aluminum foil, until the chicken is done, about 25 minutes, basting every so often.

Remove the chicken from the pan and keep warm. Sprinkle the arrowroot or cornstarch into the pan and work it in with the back of a spoon, then stir it into the pan juices until smooth. Add the remaining 1 cup pineapple juice, 2 tablespoons juice concentrate, 1/8 teaspoon cayenne, and 1/8 teaspoon curry powder. Bake at 400 degrees F. for 5 minutes, stirring often. If the mixture doesn't thicken, stir in a little more arrowroot or cornstarch and bake for a few minutes extra. If it becomes too thick, add more pineapple juice and a little more juice concentrate.

Serve over brown rice or whole wheat spaghetti. Be sure to pour some of the delicious sauce over the chicken.

One chicken breast or one thigh and drumstick is equal to 3-1/2-4 ounces of meat. If you are on a very strict diet and can only have 1-1/2 ounces of meat, remove the meat from a piece of cooked breast and cut it in half. Weigh to be sure you have just 1-1/2 ounces of meat. Serve on a plate with warm sauce from the baking dish poured over the chicken.

POULET SAUCE AUX FRUITS
(Chicken With Fruit Sauce)

Yield: 5-6 servings

This is a delightful dish to make and so impressive, but so easy.

5-6 chicken breasts
Cayenne pepper
Garlic powder
Onion powder
1 recipe for Fruit Patrician (page 222)
Cooked brown rice or brown and wild rice mixed (page 233)

Bone and skin the chicken breasts. Place each one on a board bone side up. With a meat pounder or a potato masher, flatten the breasts. Fold in three sections with the beaten side in, as you would a letter. Turn seam side down and place an inch or so apart in a nonstick baking pan. There is no need to seal them in any way. They won't come apart while baking. Sprinkle each piece with about 1/16 teaspoon of cayenne pepper, garlic powder, and onion powder. Bake for about 25 minutes 350 degrees F.

Meanwhile, prepare the Fruit Patrician. Serve the Fruit Patrician over the chicken and rice. Serve along with some steamed cauliflower florets mixed with brussels sprouts. Each breast will contain 3-1/2-4 ounces of meat.

VARIATION

Poulet Sauce Cerise (Chicken with Cherry Sauce). Prepare the chicken breasts as above, but substitute Cherry Glaze (page 223) for the Fruit Patrician. Serve along with Creamed Spaghetti Milano and steamed spinach and carrots on the side.

CHICKEN JAMBALAYA

• • • • • • • • • • • • • • • • • • • •

Yield: Eight 1-cup servings

The Cajun-style Chicken Jambalaya that you eat at restaurants, church fairs, and at the New Orleans Jazz Festival is made with chicken and sausage. Of course, sausage is out, so we will just use chicken.

1-1/2 pounds diced raw chicken
2 cups Concentrated Chicken Stock (page 58)
1/3 cup water
2-1/2 cups chopped onions
2 cups chopped green pepper
2/3 cup finely chopped carrot
2 cups uncooked brown and wild rice mixed or plain brown rice
2 tablespoons tomato paste
2 tablespoons apple juice concentrate
1 tablespoon red hot sauce (not Tabasco)
1/2 teaspoon cayenne pepper
1 teaspoon powdered or crumbled thyme
1/4 teaspoon garlic powder
2 large bay leaves
1-1/2 cups chopped celery
1 tablespoon parsley flakes

Start a day ahead by skinning and chopping the chicken into bite-sized pieces, making sure you get every bit of fat off the chicken. Make the Concentrated Chicken Stock from the neck, back, and bones. Refrigerate the stock overnight and skim the grease off.

Put the onions, green peppers, and carrots in a nonstick 5-quart pot and turn the heat on high. Saute' until the onions look brown around the edges and a little transparent. Add the chicken stock and water. Reduce the heat to low. Add the rice and all the other ingredients, including the chicken. Mix well, cover, and cook on the lowest heat for 50 minutes. Turn off the heat and let it sit covered, for 30 minutes. Stir with a fork and serve.

If divided into eight 1-cup servings each serving will contain about 4 ounces of chicken. If you want less meat, just don't use as much. It won't make a whole lot of difference in the taste.

WILD DUCK STEW

• • • • • • • • • • • • • • • • • • •

Yield: 6-8 servings

So the hunter in your family has arrived home victorious, holding up several limp, sweet, feathery little creatures. What do you do with them? I always feel just terrible, weep a little, and wonder how someone could go out into the marsh, which is walking distance from my house, and kill those beautiful, wild creatures. Then, I can't see those precious ducks having lost their lives in vain, so I plan to cook them, but first, I insist the men clean them. My husband will probably never read this recipe, so I can safely tell you that I do know how to clean a duck. Here's how.

First chop off the head, wings, and feet. Then make an incision right underneath the breast and make a hole large enough to take out the innards. At my house this is done on the edge of the bayou, and the guts go to the crabs. They love it. If you don't have a convenient bayou, use your imagination. Now, instead of plucking the feathers it is easier to just skin the duck. Get a knife just underneath the skin starting at the bottom of the breast where the incision was made. Loosen the skin and then start pulling it off. It will come off all in one piece.

You don't need the back of the duck as it has no meat worth worrying about and only serves to give the duck that wild taste, so first cut off the legs, and then hold the neck of the duck with your left hand and the breast side with your right. Pull the neck back and down and the whole back bone will come out in one piece. It takes a little strength, but if I can do it, anyone can. Just throw it away or feed it to the crabs. It is no good for stock. Cut the breast in half the long way and add to the two legs.

It doesn't matter if you have 2 or 3 different kinds of ducks. I know some people will carry on over this, but when they are stewed all together, I defy anyone to tell me which duck is which. The only kind of duck I would not mix with the others is called a poule d'eau (pull-doo) or water chicken. Instead of a bill it has a beak that looks just like a chicken's. This duck has a very fishy taste and could mess up the taste of your stew. It is only found in the bayous and marshes of Louisiana.

---

4 wild ducks
1 large white onion, chopped
1/2 large green pepper, chopped
1/2 large sweet red bell pepper, chopped
2 celery ribs and leaves, chopped
3 tablespoons whole wheat flour
Water
5 garlic cloves, chopped
2 tablespoons dried parsley flakes
1/2 teaspoon cayenne pepper
1 bay leaf
1 teaspoon powdered or crumbled thyme
1 teaspoon sage
1/4 teaspoon ground ginger
3 tablespoons apple juice concentrate
3/4 cup chablis or claret
6 large mushrooms, sliced

Wash the duck pieces very well. Spray a nonstick 5-quart pot lightly with a non-stick spray and wipe a little bit out of it if you like. Preheat the pot slightly over a medium heat. Place as many duck pieces as you can in it without them touching. When they start to sizzle turn the pieces over and over to brown. Remove the browned pieces to a bowl and add the remaining duck.

When all the duck is browned and in the bowl, immediately add the onion, peppers, and celery to the pot. You don't have to worry about wiping fat from the pot, because after these ducks have flown all the way from Canada, they have virtually no fat. They are not like those fat, lazy, grocery store ducks. If you live where wild ducks just float around on ponds, then you might have to worry about wiping fat out of the pot. Sauté the vegetables over medium heat, turning them over and over until the onions look a little brown around the edges and somewhat transparent.

Sprinkle the flour over the vegetables and stir it in, turning it over and over with the vegetables. When the flour begins to smoke, keep turning it over with the vegetables for about 20 seconds more, then quickly add 1 cup of water and stir it in well. Add another cup of water and stir. Reduce the heat to low. Add the garlic, parsley, cayenne, bay leaf, thyme, sage, ginger, juice concentrate, and wine. Return the duck to the pot. Stir and cover. Cook over a very low heat for about 3 hours. Stir occasionally and add a little water if needed. The liquid should almost cover the pieces of duck.

Add the mushrooms during the last half hour of cooking. The meat should just fall off the bones. Cook longer if it doesn't. Some birds will be tougher than others, so test each one with a sharp knife. If you want a little more edge to the taste, add more cayenne pepper, more apple juice concentrate, and a couple of tablespoons of wine.

Serve with fluffy brown rice. This could actually serve 8 people with about 2 ounces of meat per person, but more realistically, I wouldn't count on serving more than 6. Somebody is bound to want seconds. Take only a piece of breast and a leg if you are on a calorie counting diet; this will be 2-3 ounces of meat. Warn diners to watch out for tiny bones and buckshot. Try to get all the shot out, but you might miss a little piece; so be careful, you don't want to break your teeth. A green vegetable and a salad is good with this. French Rolls are good for sopping up gravy.

• FISH AND SEAFOOD •

CRAWFISH ÉTOUFFÉE

• • • • • • • • • • • • • • • • • • • •

Yield: 3-4 servings

I know some of you may never have eaten a crawfish (crawdad, to some; crayfish to others); however, in south Louisiana we eat them like wild and have beaucoup (plenty) recipes for them. I understand there are crawfish in Oregon, but according to the Cajun cooks in Louisiana who have tried them, they are not as delicate and tasty as the ones in Louisiana. If you don't live in Louisiana and you can't get them fresh, you may be able to buy Louisiana crawfish frozen at your grocery, fishmonger, or gourmet shop. I have used frozen tails in this recipe and I can guarantee, they are positively super.

If the prospect of eating a crawfish leaves you feeling a little peculiar, I won't insist. You can substitute 9 ounces of shrimp, clams, oysters, crabmeat, or chunks of any firm-fleshed white fish.

Étouffée (Cajunized) is pronounced ae-too-fay. If you make this with shrimp it is Shrimp Étouffée, etc. According to one French-English dictionary étouffée in this feminine form means simply stew.

Interestingly, the adjective, étouffant, means suffocating and étouffer, the infinitive, means to smother. Smothering and stewing would seem to be just a little bit different when it comes to cooking, but are they really?

Many people in New Orleans think that étouffée means stuffed. This goes back to the days when ladies wore tight corsets. In hot weather they would suffocate, or smother, because they were "stuffed" into their corsets. People who think étouffée means stuffed look for stuffed crawfish in their étouffée, but they never find them.

Some people don't use water to make this dish but I have seen expert restaurant cooks use water or crawfish stock made from the shells to extend the liquid. But, there again, crawfish étouffée recipes are something like gumbo recipes. There are probably a 1,000 recipes, but they all turn out to be crawfish étouffée just as gumbo always turns out to be gumbo. And like hogshead cheese, by the time a bunch of Cajuns and Creoles from New Orleans finish arguing about how to make it, the hogs have picked up and left.

---

9 ounces fresh or frozen peeled cooked crawfish tails, or 70 medium-
* size live crawfish*
1 large onion, chopped
1 large green pepper, chopped
5 celery ribs, chopped
5 garlic cloves, chopped
2 teaspoons low-sodium tamari or soy sauce
1/4 cup whole wheat flour
Water
2 teaspoons dried parsley flakes or 1/4 cup fresh parsley chopped
2 bay leaves
1 teaspoon powdered or crumbled thyme
1 tablespoon plus 1 teaspoon apple juice concentrate
3 tablespoons rosé wine
Cayenne pepper

If by chance you have live crawfish, you must purge them in salt water first. Place the crawfish in a pail and cover them with water. Add about 2 cups of salt to the water and stir. Let the crawfish sit for about 30 minutes. This takes a lot of the dirt out of them. In the meantime, bring to boil a large pot of water.

When the water is boiling rapidly, remove the crawfish from the salted water and add to the boiling water. Boil for 20 minutes, then allow them to cool in the water. Peel as you would shrimp and be sure to devein them. They are much sandier and muddier than shrimp. Refrigerate.

Combine the onion, green pepper, and celery, in a nonstick frying pan. Turn the heat on high. Add the tamari or soy sauce and sauté until the onion starts to look transparent. Add the flour and stir until it begins to smoke. Continue to stir for about 20 seconds, then immediately add a little water and keep stirring. Reduce the heat to medium. Add more water, a little at a time, stirring all the time and smoothing out any lumps in the flour. Continue adding water and stirring until you have added enough water to cover the vegetables and a little bit more. Cook, stirring constantly, until the mixture thickens. The exact amount of liquid is not important. You are aiming for a gravy about the consistency of melted ice cream. For now, though, make it thinner than that, because it is going to cook down and you want to have enough liquid to allow for evaporation.

Add the parsley, garlic, bay leaves, thyme, juice concentrate, and wine. Simmer, covered, for 2 hours. Stir often. Add water if needed.

Fifteen minutes before serving, add the crawfish, fish, shrimp, oysters or clams, and cayenne to taste. Simmer for just 15 minutes. Do not overcook or the seafood will shrink to nothing or get mushy. Serve over fluffy brown rice.

Obviously, the serving size is 3 ounces of crawfish per person if you serve 3 people. For the regression diet, reduce the amount of peeled crawfish to 4-1/2 ounces, but use the same amount of other ingredients or add a little more chopped celery (1-1-1/2 cups) to fill out the volume. The crawfish or other fish will be sparse but you will still have enough gravy to put over your rice. Or, you can make this dish as is and pick out 5 or 6 crawfish and weigh them to be exact. Broken up fish will be harder to pick out than shrimp or crawfish if you have to be exact. Just use the 4-1/2 ounces of fish, and then you won't have to worry so much about getting more than 1-1/2 ounces of meat.

SHRIMP CREOLE

• • • • • • • • • • • • • • • • • • • •

Yield: 4 servings

1 large onion, chopped
1 large green pepper, chopped (about 1-1/2 cups)
1-1/4 cups chopped celery ribs and leaves
1 small carrot, finely chopped
2 cups water
1 large tomato, chopped
2 bay leaves
2-1/2 cups cubed white potatoes
12 ounces unpeeled fresh shrimp (6 ounces fresh peeled shrimp or
    15 large fresh shrimp), or 6 ounces canned or frozen shrimp
1 cup shrimp stock (page 58) or water
1 teaspoon dried parsley flakes
4 teaspoons no-salt tomato paste
2 tablespoons apple juice concentrate
1/8 teaspoon cayenne pepper
1/2 teaspoon low-sodium tamari or soy sauce
1/8 teaspoon garlic powder
1 teaspoon powdered or crumbled thyme
1/8 teaspoon ground allspice
2 teaspoons fresh lemon juice

Combine the onion, green pepper, celery, and carrot in a non-stick frying pan. Turn the heat on high and sauté for about 6 minutes, until the onion is brown on the edges and slightly transparent. Add the water and reduce the heat. Add the tomato, bay leaves, and potatoes. Cover and simmer for 1 hour, stirring occasionally.

If you have fresh shrimp, peel and devein the shrimp and make the shrimp stock. Keep the peeled shrimp refrigerated.

After the vegetable mixture has simmered for 1 hour, add the shrimp stock or water. Simmer, uncovered, for 12 minutes. Add the parsley, tomato paste, juice concentrate, cayenne, soy sauce, garlic, thyme, allspice, and lemon juice. Stir and simmer, uncovered, for 3 minutes. Add the shrimp and simmer for 30 minutes, uncovered. Stir occasionally. Add a little water if necessary.

Let cool and refrigerate for 3-4 hours to mingle the seasonings. Reheat and serve over white or brown rice.

This recipe will serve 4 people just over 1 ounce of shrimp each.

SHRIMP JAMBALAYA

• • • • • • • • • • • • • • • • • • • •

Yield: 5 servings

1-1/4 pounds unpeeled large shrimp including the heads)
1-2/3 cups shrimp stock (page 58)
2 bay leaves
1/3 cup rosé wine
1 large onion, coarsely chopped
1 medium-size green pepper, chopped
3 celery ribs and leaves, chopped
3 medium-size tomatoes, cubed
3 tablespoons no-salt tomato paste
3 garlic cloves, finely chopped
1 teaspoon powdered or crumbled thyme
1/2 teaspoon cumin
1 teaspoon dried or 2 tablespoons chopped fresh parsley
1/2 teaspoon dried basil
1/2 teaspoon red pepper flakes
3 tablespoons apple juice concentrate
1 tablespoon low-sodium tamari or soy sauce
1 cup uncooked white rice (white tastes better with this)

Peel and devein the shrimp. Start the shrimp stock and add the bay leaves and the wine to the shrimp stock as you cook it.

While the stock is cooking, combine the onion, green pepper, and celery in a nonstick 5-quart pot. Turn the heat on high and saute', turning the vegetables over and over until the onion looks a little brown and transparent. If the stock is not ready yet, remove from heat and set aside until the stock is ready. When the stock is ready, strain and measure it. Including the wine that was added to it, you want to have 1-2/3 cups of liquid. Add water if necessary.

Pour the stock and wine mixture over the sautéed vegetables. Add the tomatoes, tomato paste, garlic, thyme, cumin, parsley, basil, red pepper, juice concentrate, and soy sauce. Stir and cover. Bring to a boil and simmer for 5 minutes. Stir in the rice and cover and simmer 35 minutes.

Uncover and gently mix in the shrimp. Cover and continue to cook on low heat for 20 minutes. Remove from the heat and let stand, covered, for 25 minutes. Fluff all the ingredients with a fork. Each 1-cup serving contains 1-1/5 ounces of shrimp.

OVEN-FRIED CATFISH WITH ONION RINGS

● ●

Yield: 2 servings

2 catfish fillets, 1-1/2 ounces each, or 1 (7-ounce) skinned and
*   deheaded catfish or rainbow trout*
1-1/2 cups skim milk
1/4 teaspoon powdered thyme
1/4 teaspoon sage
1/4 teaspoon marjoram
1/4 teaspoon cayenne pepper
1/4 teaspoon chili powder
2 teaspoons onion powder
1 teaspoon low-sodium tamari or soy sauce
1 egg white
1 large onion, cut and separated into rings
1 cup cornmeal

One 7-ounce catfish weighed without its skin and head will have about 3 ounces of meat on it. Cut it in half the short way, making the end toward the head shorter than the end toward the tail, since there is more meat toward the head. Fillets need no further cutting.

Mix the milk with thyme, sage, marjoram, 1/8 teaspoon of the cayenne pepper, and all of the chili powder, onion powder, and tamari or soy sauce. Add the egg white to milk mixture and beat.

Add the fish and onion rings to the milk mixture and marinate in the refrigerator for 2 hours or more.

Put the cornmeal in a plastic bag with the remaining 1/8 teaspoon of the cayenne pepper and shake. Add the fish, 1 piece at a time, and shake. Return each piece to the marinade for a quick dip, then immediately place in the cornmeal and shake again. Place on a non-stick pan. Place the onions in the bag with the cornmeal and shake, too. Then place the onions on the pan with the fish.

Bake the fish and onions in a preheated 400 degree F. oven. Turn the fish and onions when one side is brown. Bake until the other side is brown, 20-25 minutes in all. Serve with lemon wedges and, if you want to cheat, a little catsup. Taco Sauce is good for a Mexican taste, and it is not cheating. I also serve Oven-Fried Potatoes, which I put on a nonstick pan and bake at the same time as the fish and onions.

You have enough marinade to cover the onion rings, and you could fit several more catfish fillets in the bowl, if you like,and give each person a few less onions rings.

I freeze any leftover fish in small plastic bags and reheat frozen fish uncovered in the microwave for about 2 minutes on high. You can defrost the fish, then reheat it in an oven for about 10 minutes at 350 degrees F. It will taste almost fresh cooked.

BAKED TROUT

• • • • • • • • • • • • • • • • •

Yield: 2 servings

Buy a whole trout that weighs about 1/2 pound with the head on for each serving. It will have about 3 ounces of meat on it. You may want to buy a trout that weighs a pound or more and cut it in half to serve 2 people. Sometimes the little trout are hard to find. If you can't find trout, any other similar fresh water fish will do. Actually, you could make this recipe with sections of larger fish, such as king fish, swordfish or shark (buy baby shark — the big ones don't taste as good). Make sure the fish has been cut across the bone so some bone is still in the fish, except for shark, which is good cut any way. Do not use tuna or salmon.

2 teaspoons low-sodium tamari or soy sauce
3 tablespoons water
Juice of 1 lemon
1/4 teaspoon garlic powder
1/8 teaspoon cayenne pepper
2 small (1/2-pound) speckled trout

Mix the tamari, water, lemon juice, garlic, and cayenne in a cup or small container. Place the fish on a large sheet of aluminum foil. Draw the edges of the foil up around the fish to form a bag. Pour the seasoning over the fish. Tuck the aluminum foil up around the fish leaving an opening about 1 inch wide to let the steam out.

Place the fish in the aluminum foil on a baking pan. Bake at 300 degrees F. for 20 minutes. Open the foil and slash the fish in several places and baste with the juice around the fish. Tuck the foil up around the fish as before. Bake for 20 minutes more and serve.

This dish may seem to have a lot of salt at first glance but there is so much juice, the soy or tamari sauce becomes very diluted.

SHRIMP STUFFED WHITE SQUASH

• • • • • • • • • • • • • • • • • • • •

Yield: 3 servings

This is an extremely tasty, old-fashioned Creole dish. Even the skins of the squash are edible, unless you happened to get a tough squash, which isn't likely. The sugars in the skins become caramelized and sweet after baking. Don't miss trying them.

3 large white scalloped bush squash (patty pan)
1 medium-size onion, coarsely chopped
1 medium-size green pepper, coarsely chopped
1 cup whole wheat or Pritikin bread crumbs
1/2 teaspoon powdered or crumbled thyme
1/4 teaspoon cayenne pepper
3 ounces canned shrimp, well-rinsed, or 18 large or 30 small fresh
*   shrimp, peeled*
1/2 teaspoon red hot sauce (not Tabasco)
2 egg whites

Microwave Directions

With a knife, pierce the top of the squash in several places. Bake on high for 15 minutes. Test with a knife for tenderness. If they are still hard, cook another 2 minutes or more as needed. Remove the squash from the microwave and place on a nonstick baking pan. Let cool.

Stove Top Directions

Cook the squash in water to cover for about 45 minutes. Test with a knife for tenderness and continue cooking until tender. Carefully remove the squash from the pot and place on a nonstick baking pan. Let cool.

While the squash are cooling, combine the onion and green pepper in a nonstick frying pan. Turn the heat on high, and saute' until the onion looks transparent and slightly limp. Remove the pan from the heat. Set aside.

Cut circles out of the tops of each squash as you would if you were preparing pumpkins to make jack-o-lanterns. Lift out the circular sections. Scrape the flesh from the squash tops into the pan with the sautéed vegetables. Discard the tops. With a teaspoon, carefully scrape the flesh from the rest of the squash and add it to the pan. The seeds can be left in the mixture; they are very tender. Add the remaining ingredients to the pan and mix well.

Spoon the mixture into the squash shells. If you like, sprinkle extra bread crumbs on top, but it is not necessary. Place on the middle rack of an oven and set the temperature at 350 degrees F. Bake for 25-30 minutes and serve.

Each serving contains about 1-1/2 ounces of shrimp if you use canned shrimp, or less than 1 ounce per serving if you use fresh shrimp. Weigh the shrimp for exact measurement.

VARIATION

Meatless Stuffed White Squash. Substitute 6 ounces of low-fat cottage cheese for the shrimp. Proceed with the recipe above.

STUFFED ARTICHOKES PALERMO
• •
Yield: 2 servings (or 60 or more party servings)

You don't have to do without your stuffed artichokes just because you have put on a few pounds! You will almost swear these artichokes have olive oil in them. For a real olive oil effect, rub the plate you serve these on with some highly aromatic olive oil and it will complete the effect. No fair licking your fingers.

You can prepare these artichokes two ways. Either stuff them and leave them whole, or remove each leaf and serve them as individual bon bites *(a little something good in the mouth; an old Creole French-English expression)* at a party. *An Italian-English expression would be more appropriate I realize, but, unfortunately, I don't know one.*

29 medium-size fresh shrimp, or 3-1/2 ounces peeled canned or
*   frozen shrimp*
2 large fresh artichokes
1 medium-size onion
1 celery rib
3 large mushrooms
1 cup Concentrated Chicken Stock (page 58)
1/4 cup dry vermouth
1 tablespoon dried or 1/4 cup finely chopped fresh parsley
1/2 teaspoon powdered or crumbled thyme
1 teaspoon red hot sauce (not Tabasco)
1/2 teaspoon garlic powder
1/8 teaspoon cayenne pepper
1-1/2 teaspoons dried oregano
Water
1-1/2 cups cracked wheat bread crumbs (or use Oat Bran Bread
*   crumbs, page 53)*
2 tablespoons plus 1 teaspoon grated sapsago cheese

First, if you are using canned shrimp, rinse and soak them for 20 minutes or longer in ice water.

Next, steam the artichokes in a large covered pot in about an inch of water. Bring the water to a boil, then reduce the heat and simmer for 25-30 minutes. Don't overcook. After 20 minutes, start testing the leaves every so often. If a leaf pulls off easily and the meat on the bottom of the leaf is tender to eat, the artichoke is done. Remove from water and cool. Meanwhile prepare the filling.

Filling Directions for Stuffed Whole Artichokes

The onion, celery, and mushrooms can be chopped in a food processor. Then place the vegetables in a nonstick frying pan. Place the fresh or frozen shrimp in the food processor and chop, but not too finely. You want little chunks of shrimp. Don't chop canned shrimp.

Turn the heat on high under the frying pan and sauté the vegetables. When the onion looks brown around the edges and a little transparent, add the shrimp. Break up canned shrimp with the edge of a wooden spoon in the pan. Then add the chicken stock, vermouth, parsley, thyme, hot sauce, garlic, cayenne, and oregano. Add a little water to the food processor bowl. Swoosh it around. Add it to the frying pan. Cover and simmer until the onion and celery are tender, and shrimp are cooked, about 10 minutes. Add the bread crumbs, and sapsago cheese. Mix all together. You should have a nice, moist stuffing. If it looks a little dry and crumbly, add water. If it is too wet, add a few more bread crumbs. You don't want too many bread crumbs, though.

To stuff a whole artichoke, begin by gently pulling back the leaves of the artichoke after it has cooked and cooled. Start with the outer leaves and move toward the center. When you reach the center leaves, remove them to leave a nice cavity in the center of the artichoke. When you have pulled enough leaves from the center, you will see the "choke" part or hairy section that grows on top of the heart, or bottom as some people say. Carefully pull out the little hairs; they will come out in clumps. This leaves the heart exposed and ready for good eating.

Some people cut off the points of the leaves and you can if you want to, but it's not necessary. Carefully cut off the stem so the artichoke can sit flat. Dig out the soft, edible part of the stem, chop, and add to the filling.

Fill the cavity of the artichoke with the filling. Then put about a teaspoon of filling at the base of each leaf. When a person goes to eat a leaf, the filling will stay on the leaf and will be ready to scrape off with the teeth with the rest of the flesh. Sprinkle a few bread crumbs on top of each section of filling. It looks like grated cheese and tastes good too. Serve at room temperature.

Filling Directions for Individual Leaves

After the artichokes are cooked and cooled, pull off all the leaves. Save the sturdiest ones. Remove the "choke" from the heart. It is hairy looking and is located right on top of the heart, or bottom as some people call it. Chop the heart up and dig out a little of the middle of the stem. It has some good meat in it, too. Chop and set it aside.

The onion, celery, and mushrooms can be chopped in a food processor. Place the vegetables in a nonstick frying pan. Place fresh or frozen shrimp in the food processor and chop, but not too finely. You want little chunks of shrimp. Don't chop canned shrimp.

Turn the heat on high under the frying pan and sauté the vegetables until the onion looks brown around the edges and a little transparent. Add the shrimp (break up canned shrimp with a wooden spoon). Add the chicken stock, vermouth, parsley, thyme, hot sauce, garlic, cayenne, and oregano. Add a little water to the food processor bowl. Swoosh it around. Add it to the frying pan. Cover and simmer until the onions and celery are tender, and shrimp are cooked, about 10 minutes. Add the bread crumbs. Add the chopped artichoke and sapsago cheese. Mix all together. You should have a nice, moist stuffing. If it looks dry and crumbly, add water. If it is too wet, add a few more bread crumbs. You don't want too many bread crumbs, though.

Take about 1 teaspoon of the filling and put it on the base of each reserved leaf. Arrange them on a platter for a party.

Sprinkle a few bread crumbs over the filling of each leaf. It looks like grated cheese and tastes good too. Serve at room temperature.

If for some reason you should happen to get bitter artichokes, as I have occasionally (they are usually the small and don't have very pretty leaves), add 1 to 3 teaspoons of apple juice concentrate to your filling mixture to counteract the bitter taste.

SHIRLEY'S TUNA CASSEROLE

Yield: 6 servings

1 cup uncooked No. 1 semolina Italian-style elbow macaroni
  (whole wheat macaroni can be substituted)
2 medium-size onions, chopped
1 cup fresh or frozen sliced carrots
1 cup fresh or frozen green peas
1/2 cup water
2 (6-1/2-ounce) cans water-packed tuna, drained
2 cups skim milk
1/2 teaspoon cayenne pepper
2 tablespoons cornstarch

Cook the macaroni in 2 quarts of rapidly boiling water for about 8 minutes. If you use whole wheat macaroni, cook for 15 minutes. Drain and run some cold water through to keep it from sticking together. Set aside.

Microwave Directions

Place the onions, carrots, and peas in a 1-quart container. Add the water. Cover and cook on high for 5 minutes. Stir. Cover and cook for 4 minutes. Taste the onion. If it is still raw, cook for 3 minutes more.

Stove Top Directions

Place the onions, carrots, and peas in a 1-1/2-quart saucepan. Add the water and bring to a fast boil. Cover and cook on medium for 5 minutes. Stir and cover. Cook for 4 minutes more, until the onions are tender.

Combine the cooked vegetables and cooking liquid and the cooked macaroni in a 9-inch by 13-inch baking dish. Mix in the tuna, milk, and cayenne. Sprinkle the cornstarch over and mix in.

Bake, uncovered, at 350 degrees F for 30 minutes. Stir. Bake for 10 minutes more. Turn off the heat and let the casserole sit for 15 minutes. Sprinkle with grated sapsago cheese if desired.

Each serving contains about 2 ounces of tuna. This is nice served with a Baked Tomato and steamed cabbage.

TUNA ON TOAST

· · · · · · · · · · · · · · · · · · · ·

Yield: 3-4 servings

2 cups chicken or turkey stock
1 cup chopped onion
3 cups sliced fresh mushrooms
1 bay leaf
1 teaspoon powdered or crumbled thyme
1/8 teaspoon cayenne pepper
1 teaspoon dried or 2 tablespoons chopped fresh parsley
5 tablespoons whole wheat flour
1 (6-1/2-ounce) can water-packed tuna, drained
1 tablespoon apple juice concentrate
6-8 slices toasted commercial whole wheat or Pritikin bread

Combine the stock, onion, mushrooms, bay leaf, thyme, cayenne, and parsley in a large saucepan. Bring to a boil and reduce the heat to medium. Cook, uncovered, for 15 minutes.

With the heat still on, sprinkle about 1 tablespoon of the flour over the top and work it in with the back of a spoon and stir until smooth. Continue until you have added all the flour. Continue to cook and stir until the mixture thickens. Add the tuna and juice concentrate. Mix. Serve over toast. Pritikin rye bread tastes good with this, too.

Serve 1 or 2 slices of bread to each person. If served on 6 slices of bread, each slice of toast will hold slightly over 1 ounce of tuna.

CRAB QUICHE WITH MEDITERRANEAN SAUCE

Yield: 4 servings

8 slices commercial whole wheat or Pritikin bread
2 cups sliced fresh mushrooms
1/4 cup sliced green onions (3 small ones)
3 ounces canned white crabmeat or 1/3 cup firmly packed fresh
    crabmeat
1/4 cup low-fat cottage cheese
1 cup skim milk
6 large egg whites
1 teaspoon dried or 3 tablespoons finely chopped fresh parsley
1/4 teaspoon cayenne pepper
1/8 teaspoon garlic powder
2 tablespoons grated sapsago cheese
1-1/2 cups Mediterranean Sauce (page 219)

Remove the crusts from the bread. Place 4 of the slices in the bottom of an 8-inch by 8-inch nonstick cake pan or baking dish. Fill in any gaps between the slices with the crusts. Layer the mushrooms over the bread, then the onions, then the crabmeat, then the cottage cheese. Cover with the 4 remaining slices of bread. Fill in any gaps with more crusts.

Mix together the milk, egg whites, parsley, cayenne, and garlic. Use a blender if you have one. Pour the milk mixture slowly over the top layer of bread. Let it soak in as you go or it will run right off the top and spill on the counter. Sprinkle with sapsago cheese. Cover with aluminum foil, but don't let the foil touch the bread. Cut gashes in it to let out steam.

Bake at 350 degrees F. for 40 minutes. Let the quiche sit, covered, for about 10 minutes before serving.

About 15-20 minutes before serving time, prepare the Mediterranean Sauce. Cut the quiche in squares and serve on dinner plates with the warm Mediterranean sauce poured over. For best results, the sauce should not be reheated, but if it is necessary, reheat it on the stove over a medium heat. Add a little more milk if it is too thick. Stir constantly until it is just hot. Remove from the heat immediately.

Each person will get 1-1/2 ounces of crabmeat.

COQUILLE ST. JACQUES

• • • • • • • • • • • • • • • • • • •

Yield: 2 servings

Coquille St. Jacques (pronounced ko-keel sawn jock) is one of my favorite dishes served at Galatoire's or Brennan's in New Orleans. Naturally, they use lots of butter and heavy cream and salt; but I have "Pritikinized" the recipe.

Coquille means shell in French. If you have 2 nice big shells (about 5 inches across) to serve this in, your dish will be beautiful. If not, use 2 individual casserole dishes.

1 cup turkey or chicken stock
8 green onions, including the green part (about 1/4 pound), chopped
1 tablespoon whole wheat flour
4 tablespoons whole wheat or Pritikin bread crumbs
1/2 teaspoon powdered thyme or a little more of crumbled thyme
1/4 teaspoon red pepper flakes
1/4 teaspoon cayenne pepper or more
2 egg whites
10 large scallops (about 7 ounces)
2 teaspoons fresh lemon juice
1-1/2-2 cups Cheesy Mashed Potatoes (page 168)
2 tablespoons grated sapsago cheese
Paprika

Combine the stock and green onions in a saucepan. Bring to a boil. Reduce the heat to medium, cover, and cook gently for 5-6 minutes, until the onions are soft. Stir a few times while they cook.

Remove a few tablespoons of stock from the pot. Combine with the flour and stir until you have a smooth paste. Then add the flour mixture to the stock, stirring constantly and cooking over medium heat, until the mixture is smooth. Add 3 tablespoons of the bread crumbs, the thyme, red pepper, and cayenne. Taste. You might want another 1/8 teaspoon of cayenne. Mix in the egg whites. Remove from the heat and add the scallops and lemon juice.

Divide the mixture between 2 shells or 2 little casserole dishes. Sprinkle the remaining 1 tablespoon of bread crumbs over the tops. Place on a baking pan and bake at 400 degrees F. for 10 minutes. Remove from the oven.

If you have a pastry bag, fit it with a large decorator tip, fill with

---

the potatoes, and flute the potatoes all around the edges of the little casseroles or to the edge of the shells. Leave the center empty. Spoon the potatoes on if you don't have the pastry bag. Make little peaks in the potatoes as you would with meringue. Sprinkle with the sapsago cheese and a little paprika. Return to oven for 10 minutes more. Then switch to the broiler and broil for 3 minutes until the potatoes have brown tips. Serve immediately with a lemon wedge, a green vegetable, and a salad.

This makes about 3-1/2 ounces of scallops per person. For exact measurements, weigh the scallops before putting them in the shells or casserole dishes.

OYSTERS VENEZIA

• • • • • • • • • • • • • • • • • • • •

Yield: 4 servings

This recipe is based on the Italian-style recipes made in a few restaurants in New Orleans and by the Minacapellis who own a super resturant and dinner theater in Slidell, Louisiana. Joe's wife, Nellie, really knows how to cook this one, though not Pritikin style.

Slidell is across Lake Pontchartrain from New Orleans, and Lake Pontchartrain is where all these good shrimp and crabs come from, but not "dem ersters" as many people in "Nawlins" say. Oysters come from farther out nearer the Gulf of Mexico where the water is saltier.

The restaurants use only olive oil, bread crumbs, seasonings, Parmesan cheese, and oysters in this recipe. I added all the other ingredients to doctor it up since you can't have the olive oil or salt. It comes out very similar in taste and even tastes better warmed over the next day.

1 cup Concentrated Chicken Stock (page 58)
1 (10-ounce) jar oysters or about 2 dozen fresh oysters with
*   their liquor*
1 cup chopped onion
1/2 cup chopped green pepper
2 celery ribs, no leaves, coarsely chopped
1 teaspoon dried parsley flakes
4 slices commercial whole wheat or Pritikin bread (enough to make
*   2 cups of bread crumbs)*
1/2 teaspoon cumin
2 teaspoons dried oregano
1 teaspoon banana flakes
1/8 teaspoon cayenne pepper
1 teaspoon onion powder or dried onion flakes
1/2 teaspoon garlic powder
1 cup sliced fresh mushrooms
2 tablespoons grated sapsago cheese

Prepare the chicken stock a day in advance. Refrigerate the stock overnight. Skim off any grease.

Pour the stock into a 2-cup measuring cup along with the liquor from the oysters. Add enough water, if necessary, to make 1-1/2 cups.

Pour the stock and oyster juice into a large saucepan. Add the onion, green pepper, celery, and parsley. Cover and simmer until the onion is tender, 5-6 minutes after the liquid comes to a boil.

Break the bread slices up and combine with cumin, oregano, banana flakes, cayenne, onion powder or flakes, and garlic in a food processor or a blender. Process to make crumbs. A food processor works best. Measure. If you come out with less than 2 cups, make more crumbs with more bread and mix with the other crumbs.

Spread 1 cup of crumbs on the bottom of a nonstick 8-inch by 8-inch baking dish. Spread the mushrooms over the crumbs. Then layer the oysters over that.

Drain the onion, green pepper, celery, and parsley, reserving the liquid. Layer the onion, green pepper, celery, and parsley over the oysters. Now layer the remaining cup of bread crumbs over the vegetables. Pour the remaining liquid from cooked vegetables all around on top of the bread crumbs. Sprinkle with the sapsago cheese.

Bake, uncovered, at 350 degrees F. on the middle shelf for 35 minutes. Transfer to the broiler and broil for about 3 minutes to crisp the top. Check after every minute. When the top looks nice and brown, it is done.

This will serve 4 people slightly more than 2 ounces of oysters each.

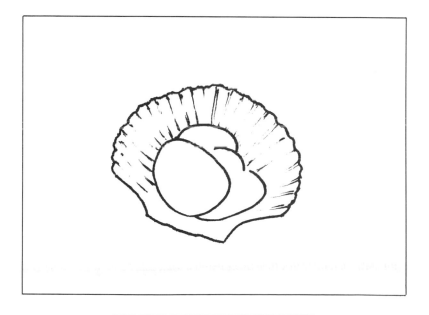

EGG ROLLS

Yield: 2-4 servings

These egg rolls taste as good or better than any you might eat in an oriental restaurant. Instead of the usual egg roll wrappers, use lumpia wrappers, which are sometimes called pastry wrappers. The ingredients listed on the package of the wrappers should include just flour, water, and salt. If you can't find lumpia wrappers, try rice papers. They must be dipped in water before you fill them. Use 2 rice papers together. The pastry wrappers are easier to work with, are more flaky, and are more successful. If you can't find either, ask Newton Food Products Mfg. Co., 84 R. Delfin St., Valenzuela, Metro Manila, Philippines, for pastry wrappers.

1 large white or yellow onion, coarsely chopped
1 large green pepper, coarsely chopped
1 teaspoon low-sodium tamari or soy sauce
2 egg whites, slightly beaten
3 1/2 ounces peeled fresh shrimp (about 10 large unpeeled shrimp)
10 sheets large lumpia wrappers (or 8 round rice papers)

Combine the onion and green pepper in a nonstick frying pan. Turn the heat on high and sauté, stirring constantly. When the onion begins to look transparent, add soy sauce and continue to stir. The onion should start to look a little brown. Reduce heat to medium. Continue to stir until the onion is almost cooked. Taste. It should still be just a little crunchy. Add the egg white and stir until cooked and white. Add the whole shrimp and remove the pan from the heat.

Pile 5 lumpia wrappers on top of each other on a large nonstick cookie sheet. Place half of the shrimp mixture in the center. Roll the wrappers around the mixture and place seam side down on a cake rack on top of a cookie sheet. There is no need to seal the seam in any way. The rolls will stay together just fine after they are cooked. Cut the roll in half and move the halves about an inch apart. Do the same thing again with the rest of the mixture.

If you have rice papers, dip them in water, then fill and roll them as described for the lumpia wrappers.

Bake, uncovered, in a preheated 350 degree F. oven for about 15 minutes until lightly brown. Check every 5 minutes. You can set the rolls on a nonstick pan instead of on the cake racks, but the racks make the rolls extra crispy. When the rolls are brown, serve immediately with Sweet and Sour Sauce and Chinese Mustard Sauce.

This recipe makes 4 nice fat, crisp egg rolls. One per person may be enough; but they are so good, you had better double this recipe. Each egg roll contains less than 1 ounce of shrimp.

• BEEF •

SWISS STEAK

• • • • • • • • • • • • • • • • • • • •

Yield: 4-5 servings

1 pound round steak, sliced 1/2 inch thick
Whole wheat flour
Cayenne pepper
Water
1 bay leaf
1/4-1/2 teaspoon powdered or crumbled thyme
4 teaspoons low-sodium tamari or soy sauce
1 large onion, chopped

Trim off as much fat as possible from the steak. Place in a nonstick frying pan. Sprinkle flour over and rub in the flour with a fork. Turn the steak over and set the heat on high. Sprinkle the other side with flour, then sprinkle lightly with cayenne. Brown the steak on both sides.

Add enough water to almost cover the browned steak. Add the bay leaf, thyme, and tamari or soy sauce. Stir. Sprinkle in the onion (some on top of the steak and some in the water) and cover. Reduce the heat and simmer for at least 2 hours. Check and stir and move the steak around fairly often. If the water level goes down, add more.

Slice into serving size-portions and serve with the gravy over cooked brown rice. For a 1-1/2-ounce serving piece, cut off a section 1 inch by about 3 inches. Weigh to be sure. If you are really very scrupulous about the fat, let the pan with meat and gravy sit in the refrigerator overnight. The next day, skim off every bit of grease, then serve. It might even taste better than it would have the first day.

BROILED STEAK AND ALLIGATOR STEW

Sprinkle any kind of steak with garlic powder and cayenne pepper and broil as usual. You won't miss the salt. Some people squeeze lemon juice over too. You might love it that way.

One old fellow I know, who uses lemon juice over steak, stews alligator meat in tomato gravy. Just the tail meat; it's the most tender. I won't give you a complete recipe for alligator stew, but if you should hunt alligator and catch one, cook it in Italian tomato sauce, substituting bay leaves and thyme for cumin and oregano.

I refuse to discuss how to skin the alligator. If you haven't got an available Cajun to ask, I'm afraid I can't help you. How do you catch an alligator? Just get yourself a nice fat chicken and put it on a big hook that is attached to a rope. Tie the rope to something sturdy and dangle the chicken above the water. The alligator will jump up to get the chicken and you've got him.

Back to the steak. A section of steak about 3 inches by 1 inch by 1/2 inch thick is roughly 1-1/2 ounces of meat. Don't worry if you weigh a section this size and it is a little heavier; it will be lighter after it is broiled. It is better to broil a whole steak and then divide it because it cooks better that way. But you can broil a tiny piece. Have the broiler very hot and don't broil too long because the meat will get as hard as a rock.

Alligator comes off the bones in little chunks, so you will just have to weigh it out after you debone it. In case you have never eaten alligator before, it tastes similar to chicken.

HOME-STYLE BEEF STEW

Yield: 7-8 servings

There is nothing like a plate of beef stew to make you feel like you have really had a good meal. This stew turns out just delicious.

1-1/2 pounds very lean stew meat
3 medium-size onions, chopped
1 small green pepper, chopped
3 tablespoons whole wheat flour
Water
4 medium-size Irish potatoes, peeled and cut in large pieces

5 large carrots, cut in 1-inch pieces
6 large mushrooms, sliced
1 tablespoon dried parsley
1 teaspoon garlic powder
2 bay leaves
1/2 teaspoon cayenne pepper
1 tablespoon apple juice concentrate
1/2 teaspoon powdered or crumbled thyme
1/2 cup fresh or frozen green peas

Remove any visible fat from the meat and cut into 1-inch cubes. Cover the bottom of a 5-quart nonstick pot with some of the meat; don't allow the pieces to touch. Turn the heat to medium high. Brown the meat, stirring occasionally. If the pot starts to smoke, reduce the heat. When the first batch of meat is brown, remove to a bowl or plate and brown the remaining meat. If the heat is not browning the meat quickly, turn the heat up to avoid steaming the meat. Add the meat to the first batch and set aside.

Pour off any grease that formed. Wipe out the pot with a paper towel.

Next, toss in the onions and green pepper and saute' until the onions begin to get a little brown and look transparent. Sprinkle the flour over the vegetables and mix it in by turning the vegetables over and over as you cook over a high heat. When the flour begins to smoke, continue turning the flour and vegetables over for about 20 seconds more. Add a little water immediately and reduce the heat. Add more water a little at a time, stirring constantly.

When you have added enough water to calm the cooking down so it is not boiling as fast, add the meat, potatoes, carrots, mushrooms, parsley, garlic, bay leaves, cayenne, and juice concentrate. Add enough water to cover everything and cover the pot. Simmer for 2-3 hours, until the meat is very tender. Add the thyme and peas and simmer for 30 minutes.

It's best to let this sit overnight in the refrigerator to let any grease harden on top, then skim it off, reheat, and eat.

This makes a big pot of stew, which is delicious served over brown rice. If you are very strict about your meat serving sizes, take a few cubes of meat after it has cooked and weigh. Put that on your rice and then serve yourself some of the rest of the stew over that.

GYRO SANDWICHES

Yield: 13 sandwiches (13 servings)

2 pounds very lean ground beef
1 cup finely chopped onion
4 teaspoons banana flakes
1/2 teaspoon allspice
1/2 teaspoon nutmeg
1/2 teaspoon anise seeds
1/2 teaspoon sage
1/2 teaspoon cayenne pepper
1/2 teaspoon dried basil
1/2 teaspoon paprika
2 teaspoons dried parsley flakes
1 teaspoon garlic powder
2 large egg whites
2 slices commercial whole wheat or Pritikin bread
13 pita breads
Tomatoes
Lettuce
Imitation Mayonnaise (page 185)

If you have a large food processor, combine the meat, onion, banana flakes, seasonings, and egg white in the bowl of the food processor fitted with a chopping blade. Wet the bread, squeeze it out, and add it to the processor. Turn on the processor. Chop everything until the meat looks as fine as liver cheese. If you have a normal-size food processor, divide the ingredients in half and perform this step in 2 batches.

Place the meat in a 9-inch by 13-inch baking dish. Form a loaf that looks like a large French bread.

If you don't have a food processor, you can still make this by mixing up the ingredients and forming a loaf, but the texture won't be as fine. With the processor, the meat appears to be very tender roast beef after it is cooked.

Microwave Directions
Microwave, uncovered, on bake, or 60 percent power, or a medium setting for 45 minutes.

Oven Directions

Bake, uncovered, at 350 degrees F. for about 1 hour or until cooked through.

While the meat bakes, shred some lettuce and slice some tomatoes. This recipe will make 13 gyro sandwiches containing 2 ounces of meat each, so decide how many sandwiches you want to make and prepare as much lettuce and tomatoes as you will need. Also make some Imitation Mayonnaise. If you want to make 13 sandwiches all at once, make 5 batches of the Imitation Mayonnaise.

When the meat is done, let it sit out of the oven for about 10 minutes, then slice very thin slices from across the top. Do not slice down. If you have ever seen cooks in restaurants slicing the meat for gyros, you will have noticed that they sliced off the side of the loaf. Their loaf is cooked on a spit in a upright positon. Yours is horizontal, so their side is your top. Weigh the slices if you are on a strict diet.

Cut the pita bread in half for 2 pockets. I use bread that is 5-6 inches in diameter. Stuff some meat in each pocket, then some lettuce and some tomato. Put a dollop of Imitation Mayonnaise in each pocket. I like my Gyros with only the meat hot. My husband likes to put his whole sandwich in the microwave for 40 seconds on high and to heat it through. You can heat them in a covered dish in a preheated 350 degree F. oven but it takes 15-20 minutes.

Serve with steamed spinach and some mixed peas and whole kernel corn.

To freeze, slice off 2-ounce servings, and place in small plastic bags. Put the small bags in one large one and mark it "Gyros." Reheat the frozen meat in the microwave for 1-2 minutes or place in aluminum foil and heat in an oven for 10-15 minutes at 450 degrees F.

TACOS

• • • • • • • • • • • • • • • • • • •

Yield: 5-6 servings

Meat and Seasoning

1-1/2 pounds very lean ground beef
1-3/4 cups water
1/4 cup yellow cornmeal
1 cooked new potato, peeled, or 1/4 cup firmly packed cooked potatoes
1 tablespoon onion powder
1/2 teaspoon garlic powder
1/2 teaspoon paprika
2 teaspoons chili powder
Mock Kitchen Bouquet (page 227)
8 drops Tabasco sauce
2 teaspoons low-sodium tamari or soy sauce
1/4 teaspoon cayenne pepper
6 tablespoons apple juice concentrate

Brown the beef in a nonstick pan and drain off all the grease. Place the meat in a colander and drain some more. Then toss the meat on some paper towels to drain further. Pat all over with more paper towels. Wipe or wash the pan out to remove any grease remaining. Return the meat to the pan.

Mix 3/4 cup of the water with the other ingredients in a blender, and liquify. Pour into the pan with the meat and mix. Pour the remaining 1 cup water in the blender and swoosh it around to remove any remaining seasoning. Pour it in the pan with the meat. If there is still a little more seasoning left in the blender, add a little more water, swoosh again, and add that too. Simmer, uncovered, stirring every 5-10 minutes, for 30 minutes. Add more water if the mixture starts to dry out. It should be pretty thick when finished.

Taco Sauce

1 tablespoon cornstarch
3/4 cup water
3 tablespoons no-salt tomato paste
1-1/2 teaspoons + 7 drops Tabasco sauce
3 tablespoons vinegar
4-1/2 teaspoons apple juice concentrate
4-1/2 teaspoons chili powder

1-1/2 teaspoons garlic powder
3/4 teaspoons onion powder

Microwave Directions

In a 1-quart container, combine the cornstarch and water, stirring and blending slowly until the cornstarch is free from lumps. Place in microwave for 1-1/2 minutes on high, then stir well. Return to the microwave for another 1-1/2 minutes, stir again. Measuring carefully, add all other ingredients and mix. Serve.

Stove Top Directions

Frankly, I think the sauce is easier to make on top the stove than in the microwave. In a small saucepan, place the cornstarch. Add the water, stirring and blending it in slowly, until the mixture is free from lumps. Cook over high heat, stirring constantly. As it heats, it will look like it isn't going to do anything, but keep stirring and suddenly the mixture will thicken. It will look almost clear when it has thickened. Cook for 20-25 seconds more, stirring constantly, and then remove from heat. Mix in all the other ingredients and serve.

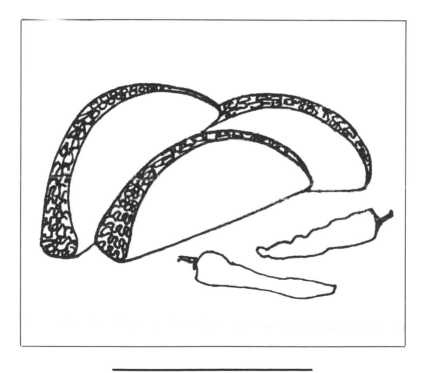

Tortillas

(8-ounce) packages frozen corn tortillas (24 tortillas)

Line every other wire in your oven rack with aluminum foil to make them a little broader. Bend each defrosted tortilla over a foil-covered wire with the ends hanging down. Bake in a preheated 300 degree F. oven until toasted, 3-5 minutes. Check them before 3 minutes, and watch them very closely or they will burn. They are really temperamental. The ones closest to the heat toast first.

Sometimes, depending on the tortillas, they break off and fall to the bottom of the oven; but usually this method works well. If the tortillas tend to crack at the edges when you bend them, they will probably break all the way as they begin to toast. In that case, instead of bending them, simply lie them flat across your oven racks to make a flat taco or tostado. You can skip lining the racks with aluminum foil, too, and they eat just as good as tacos. Just pile everything on top.

Vegetable and Cheese Filling

1 large onion, diced
2 medium-size tomatoes, diced
1 head of lettuce, shredded
1 (12-ounce) carton (1-3/4 cups) low-fat cottage cheese

Place the prepared vegetables on a platter in an attractive design, or place them in separate dishes. Cottage cheese could be placed in the center of the platter with a little curly parsley at its edge here and there.

Everybody can assemble their taco as they please. To get the most flavor, I suggest filling the toasted tortillas with the meat filling, then lettuce, tomatoes, onions, cottage cheese, and taco sauce over all. This recipe will feed 5 people generously and 6 people normally.

Each taco contains 1 ounce of meat if the meat and seasoning is divided among 24 taco shells.

PARTY MEATBALLS

• •

Yield: About 65 meat balls

You can make these meatballs ahead and store them all together in a plastic bag in the freezer. Then take them out, make the Italian Tomato Sauce, heat the meatballs in the sauce, and keep them warm in a slow cooker set on low or a large food warmer. Serve with toothpicks at a party, not over your good pastel oriental rug, as I did the first time I served them. Now I put them in the kitchen where it's safer.

If you would like these for dinner, they weigh about 1 ounce each, so 3-4 meatballs and some gravy over spaghetti would be considered a serving.

4 pounds very lean ground beef
4 egg whites
4 slices commercial whole wheat or Pritikin bread
2 tablespoons onion powder
1 teaspoon cayenne pepper or more
4 teaspoons garlic powder
Italian Tomato Sauce (page 185)(multiply the recipe by 4)

Put half the ground beef in a food processor. Add 2 of the egg whites and half the seasonings. Hold 2 slices of bread under the faucet to wet it. Squeeze the water out of the bread, then break it up over the meat. Turn on the processor and let it chop the meat and blend the ingredients until it makes a ball. Repeat with the remaining meat, egg whites, seasonings, and bread. If you have an extra large food processor, you can do this in one batch. Or just mix up all the ingredients by hand. However, the cutting blade on the processor grinds the meat very finely, and the meat balls hold together much better.

Roll walnut-size balls between the palms of your hands. Set the balls on a nonstick broiler rack or on a nonstick pan. Bake in a preheated 450 degree F. oven for 15-20 minutes. Turn as the meatballs brown on one side. When brown on both sides, remove and drain on paper towels 4 sheets thick. There should be very little grease, but the paper towels give extra insurance.

Combine the meatballs with the Italian Tomato Sauce, heat, and serve.

LASAGNA

• • • • • • • • • • • • • • • • • • • •

Yield: 8 servings

This is a great dish to fix when you feel like cooking. Make plenty. Then when the lasagna is cold, cut it into serving-sized squares and freeze in individual sandwich bags or seal-a-meal bags. When you absolutely don't have time to cook or can't stand another day of cooking from scratch, take out as many servings as you need. Place them on plates covered with plastic wrap and reheat in the microwave for 10 minutes on high, or wrap in aluminum foil and place in the oven. Set the heat on 400 degrees F. and heat for about 20 minutes or until heated through.

3/4 cup low-fat cottage cheese
1/4 medium-size onion
1 pound lean ground beef
1 large onion
1 large green pepper
1 carrot
1 celery rib
7 large mushrooms
2 small zucchini
2 cups water
1/2 cup no-salt tomato paste
1/2 cup rosé wine
1/2 cup Roast Beef Gravy I (page 228) or II (page 230)
1 tablespoon grape or apple juice concentrate
1 teaspoon dried oregano
2 teaspoons dried or 1/4 cup coarsely chopped fresh parsley,
    loosely packed
1/4 teaspoon red pepper flakes or more to taste
1/2 teaspoon cumin
1-1/2 teaspoons dried basil
1/2 teaspoon garlic powder or 5 garlic cloves, chopped
12 whole wheat lasagna noodles
Sapsago cheese

Combine the cottage cheese and 1/4 onion in a blender and blend until cheese is half as lumpy as normal. Refrigerate.

Brown the ground beef in a nonstick frying pan. Drain in a colander and then on paper towels. Put in a bowl, and wipe out or wash the pan.

Chop the remaining large onion and green pepper rather coarsely, then chop the carrot and celery very finely, preferably in a food processor. Slice the mushrooms and zucchini.

Combine the onion, pepper, carrot, celery, and mushrooms in the frying pan. Turn the heat on high, and saute' until the onion looks brown around the edges and a little transparent. Add the water, tomato paste, wine, gravy, and juice concentrate. Then add the oregano, parsley, red pepper flakes, and cumin. Add the drained, browned ground meat. Cover and cook over low heat for 2 hours. Check often and stir. Add more water if the sauce becomes too thick. During the last 10 minutes of cooking, add the basil and garlic.

When sauce is almost done, start heating a large pot of water for the noodles. When the water comes to a fast boil, add the noodles and stir. Stir again in 5 minutes. Cook whole wheat noodles until very soft; otherwise they taste a little grainy. They should be done in about 15 minutes. Drain in a colander and cool by running a little cold water through them. Now you are ready to assemble.

In a 9-inch by 13-inch baking dish, layer the ingredients this way: sauce, pasta, sauce, cottage cheese mix, zucchini, sauce, pasta, and sauce.

Bake the lasagna at 350 degrees F. for 1 hour or until bubbly. Check after the first 20 minutes and often thereafter. No need to cover. Let sit for about 10 minutes before serving. Cut into squares and sprinkle each square with a teaspoon of grated sapsago cheese.

If the lasagna is divided into 8 servings, each serving will contain 2 ounces of meat.

MOUSSAKA

• • • • • • • • • • • • • • • • • • • •

Yield: 8 servings

The potato base and meringue topping are really special.

Meat Mixture

2 large Irish potatoes
1 large eggplant
1/2 teaspoon cayenne pepper
2 pounds lean ground beef
1 cup chopped onions
1 (6-ounce) can salt-free tomato paste
3/4 cup water or beef stock
1/2 teaspoon garlic powder
1/2 teaspoon cinnamon
3/4 teaspoon dried oregano
4 slices commercial whole wheat bread made into crumbs (use food processor)

Boil or bake the potatoes, let cool, then peel.

While the potatoes are cooking, slice the eggplant the long way into 1/4-inch-thick slices. Do not peel. Place the slices on a nonstick pan and sprinkle with 1/4 teaspoon of the cayenne. Broil until lightly brown in the oven or broiler. Turn once. Check every 3 minutes or so.

While the potatoes and eggplant cook, brown the ground beef in a nonstick frying pan. Drain off any grease. Place the meat in a colander and drain further, then place on paper towels and blot with additional paper towels. Wipe or wash out the frying pan. Add the onions to the pan and turn the heat on high. Saute' until the onions look a little transparent. Return the meat to the pan and stir in tomato paste, water or stock, garlic powder, cinnamon, oregano, and remaining 1/4 teaspoon of the cayenne.

Spray a 9-inch by 13-inch baking dish with a nonstick spray or use a nonstick baking pan.

Slice the potatoes 1/8-1/4 inch thick.

Cover the bottom of the pan with the potato slices. Sprinkle the potatoes with half of the bread crumbs. Place half the eggplant slices over potatoes and crumbs. Spread the meat mixture over the eggplant. Place the remaining eggplant slices over meat. Sprinkle with the remaining bread crumbs. Set aside and prepare the cheese topping.

Cheese Topping

8 egg whites
2 cups skim milk
5 tablespoons whole wheat flour
1/2 teaspoon nutmeg
1 cup plus 3 tablespoons low-fat cottage cheese
1/4 cup grated sapsago cheese

Beat the egg whites until stiff. Set aside.
Mix the milk, nutmeg, and flour in a blender.

Microwave Directions

Pour the milk, nutmeg, and flour mixture into a 2-quart container. Cook in the microwave for 5 minutes on high, stirring after each minute until smooth and thickened.

Stove Top Directions

Pour the milk, nutmeg, and flour mixture into a 2-quart saucepan or double boiler, and cook over medium heat, stirring constantly, until thickened.

Add the cottage cheese and sapsago cheese to the flour-milk mixture. Gently fold the mixture into egg whites. Spread over the top of the casserole. Bake at 350 degrees F. until the top browns, about 40 minutes. Serve in squares and sprinkle with the sapsago cheese.

This is a wonderful dish to freeze. After it has been refrigerated, cut into squares the size of sandwich bags. Scoop the squares into sandwich or seal-a-meal bags and freeze. You can have many hearty meals put away like this. To reheat in a microwave, place on a serving plate, cover with plastic wrap, and heat on a medium setting for 10 minutes. Or reheat covered with aluminum foil in oven at 350 degrees F. for 20-30 minutes. There is no need to defrost first. This goes beautifully with a salad.

Divided into 8 servings, each portion contains 4 ounces of meat. For less meat, reduce the ground beef to 1 pound and substitute a 12-ounce carton (1-3/4 cups) of low-fat or dry curd cottage cheese. Just add the cottage cheese to the sauce along with the browned ground beef.

STUFFED MIRLITON

• • • • • • • • • • • • • • • • • • • •

Yield: 2 servings

At one time mirlitons (pronounced milly-tawns by the New Orleans locals) were a vegetable that could be found growing only in people's backyards. Then grocery stores recently started to sell Mexican imports under the name chayotes, or vegetable pears. They are a member of the gourd family, known to botanists as the "one-seeded cucumber."

Mirlitons have a much finer and sweeter flavor than any of the other squashes. They can be stewed or boiled whole and cubed, and the cooked flesh used in salads. Look for a chartreuse-colored, pear-shaped vegetable. They are slightly larger than most pears and a little flatter.

Select the female mirliton because the skin is more tender than the male's and can be eaten along with the stuffing. The male has thorn-like projections all over the bottom. The female will be practically smooth all over. You can use a male if you can't find a female, but it might be tough.

1 female mirliton
3 ounces lean ground beef
1/2 cup chopped onion
1/2 cup cooked brown rice (page 233)
1/8 teaspoon anise seeds
1/16 teaspoon allspice
1/4 teaspoon crumbled or powdered thyme
2 teaspoons dried or 3 tablespoons finely chopped fresh parsley
1/4 teaspoon dried oregano
1 teaspoon red hot sauce (not Tabasco)
1/8 teaspoon garlic powder or dried chopped garlic
2 egg whites
2 teaspoons grated sapsago cheese

Microwave Directions

Cut the mirliton in half and place the halves together facing each other. Bake on high for 7 minutes. Let it cool.

Stove Top Directions

Place the mirliton whole in a pot and cover with water. Boil for

25-30 minutes, until tender. Pierce with a knife to test. Cut in half the long way and let it cool.

While the mirliton is cooling, place the ground meat in a frying pan, turn the heat on high, and brown. Drain in a colander, place on paper towels, and pat with additional paper towels. Wipe out the pan with more paper towels.

In the same pan, sauté the onion over a high heat until the the onion looks a little transparent and a little brown at the edges. Remove from the heat. Add the meat and the rice to the pan. Mix well.

With a teaspoon scrape the pulp from the mirliton. Add it to the pan. Save the seed. You can chop it and add it to a salad or eat it right then and there. It has a nice, nutty flavor.

Mix in the anise, allspice, thyme, parsley, oregano, hot sauce, and garlic. Place the pan over medium heat and mix in the egg whites, stirring constantly until they turn white. Remove from the heat.

Place the mirliton shells on a nonstick baking pan and stuff with the filling. Don't worry about having too much filling. Just keep piling it on a patting it down. It will fit. Sprinkle grated sapsago cheese over each shell. Pat it a little as you go to keep it from falling off. Cover loosely with aluminum foil to let some steam escape. Bake at 350 degrees F. for 25 minutes. Remove the foil and bake for another 5 minutes. Each mirliton will contain 1-1/2 ounces of meat.

VARIATION

Shrimp Stuffed Mirliton. Use 4 ounces of whole fresh peeled shrimp (about 8 or 9 ounces with the shells) or use frozen ones. You can also use 3 ounces of canned shrimp, rinsed and soaked in ice water. For seasoning use 1/2 cup chopped onions, 1/2 teaspoon crumbled or powdered thyme, 2 teaspoons dried parsley flakes, 1/8 teaspoon garlic powder, 1 teaspoon red hot sauce (not Tabasco), and 2 teaspoons sapsago cheese.

Prepare the mirliton as directed above. Sauté the onions, add the pulp and all the seasonings, except the cheese, then the shrimp. Add the 2 egg whites and let them cook over medium heat until white. Fill the shells and bake as directed above.

Each shell will contain about 1-1/2 ounces of shrimp.

STUFFED GREEN PEPPERS

Yield: 2 servings

3 ounces very lean ground beef
1 cup chopped onions
1/2 teaspoon low-sodium tamari or soy sauce
1 cup cooked brown rice or brown and wild rice (page 233)
1/4 teaspoon cayenne pepper
1/2 teaspoon garlic powder
1 teaspoon dried or 1 tablespoon chopped fresh parsley
1/2 teaspoon chili powder
1/3 cup water
1 egg white
2 green peppers
Sapsago cheese

Brown the meat in a nonstick frying pan. Drain, then pat with paper towels. Wipe out the pan or wash it. Return the meat to the pan. Turn heat on high. Add onions and tamari or soy sauce and sauté until the onions look a little bit transparent. Reduce the heat to medium and add the rice, cayenne, garlic, parsley, chili powder, and water. Mix and try to incorporate the caramelized leavings at the bottom of the pan. Mix in the egg white. Remove from heat.

Remove the stems and seeds from the peppers and discard. Stuff the mixture into the cavity of each pepper. Sprinkle each with sapsago cheese. Place in a nonstick pan and bake, uncovered, at 350 degrees F. 30 minutes. Cover with foil and bake 15 minutes more. Each serving contains 1-1/2 ounces of meat.

VARIATION

Meatless Stuffed Peppers. Substitute 1/2 cup low-fat cottage cheese for the meat. Mix it in, just before stuffing the peppers.

JAMBALAYA AU CONGRI

Yield: Twelve 1-cup servings

Black-eyed peas (page 90)
4 cups cooked brown rice (page 233)
6 ounces lean ground beef

Combine the cooked black-eyed peas and rice.

Brown the ground beef, drain, and pat with paper towels. Add to the peas. Mix up very well. It will be rather soupy. Serve the congri in a bowl and eat with a spoon or on a plate and eat with a fork. Serve some whole wheat bread for sopping up the gravy. Green peas, carrots, and cabbage go well with this, too.

There is 1/2 ounce of meat in each 1-cup serving.

• PORK •

BREADED PORK CHOPS

• • • • • • • • • • • • • • • • • • •

Yield: 6 servings

Pork is not a preferred animal food on the Pritikin diet, but I love my breaded pork chops and serve them once in a while.

4 slices Pritikin or commercial whole wheat bread
1 teaspoon powdered or crumbled dried thyme
1 teaspoon dried marjoram
1/4 teaspoon cayenne pepper
1 egg white
Skim milk
6 pork chops, each 1/2 inch thick

Break up the bread slices. Combine them in a food processor with the thyme, marjoram, and cayenne. Process to make bread crumbs. You can also make bread crumbs in a blender, but it is not as easy.

Measure the egg white. Combine with an equal amount of milk and mix well. Trim all fat off the pork chops. Dip them first in the egg-milk mixture, then in the crumbs, and pat the crumbs in on both sides. Place the chops on a nonstick baking pan. Press any extra crumbs onto the tops of the chops.

Take a piece of aluminum foil about 2 feet by 1 foot, and wad it up to make a roll about a foot long. Place it on the back of the rack in the oven to form a "pillow." Place the pan of pork chops in the oven with the "pillow" under one end so the pan is tilted. This is to make sure that if there is any grease left on your pork chops, it will collect at the front of the pan and your chops won't sit in it. Bake at 450 degrees F. about 25 minutes. Turn once

Each chop will contain 3-1/2-4 ounces of meat.

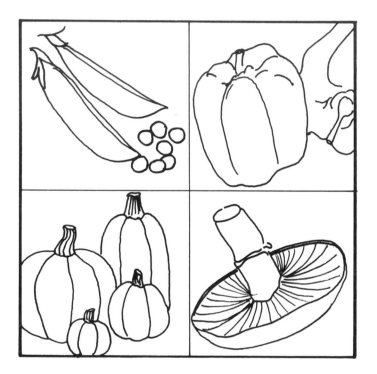

CHAPTER 7

MORE VEGETABLES

THE VEGETABLES IN THIS CHAPTER ARE VERY TASTY, TRY them without the margarine or butter. I think you will be surprised by how good they taste.

OVEN-FRIED POTATOES

Yield: 1 serving

1 large Irish potato
Cayenne pepper

Microwave Directions

Prick the potato in several places and bake in the microwave for 7 minutes. Let it cool.

Peel the potato, then cut it up as if you were making French fries.

Lay the slices in a nonstick baking pan. Sprinkle your "fries" lightly with cayenne. Place in a regular oven and bake at 350 degrees F. for 10-15 minutes. Turn once. They should be light brown.

Oven Directions

Peel the potato and cut it up as if you were making French fries. Place the slices on a nonstick baking pan and sprinkle lightly with cayenne pepper. Bake at 350 degrees F. for 25-30 minutes or until the potatoes are cooked through and light brown.

FRESH MASHED POTATOES

• • • • • • • • • • • • • • • • • • • •

Yield: 4 servings

This explanation of how to cook and mash potatoes is for those people who haven't mashed potatoes in years, since the invention of instant. I had forgotten how good fresh mashed potatoes tasted until I used this recipe. What an improvement!

3 large Irish potatoes
Skim milk
1/2 teaspoon dried basil

Peel the potatoes and cut into large pieces. In a large pot, cover the potatoes with water and bring to a boil. I like to use a Corning Ware or similar decorative pot so I can serve the potatoes in it right from the stove. Boil for 10-15 minutes, until the potatoes are very tender. Pierce with a knife to check. Drain off the water.

Mash the potatoes with a potato masher. Add enough milk to make the potatoes fluffy and creamy. Add the basil. Taste. You will be surprised how good these taste. Plain unsalted potatoes really need that basil.

If you have some Roast Beef Gravy I or II or chicken gravy (from Country Chicken Stew,) or Brown Turkey Gravy, pour that over and serve.

Variation

Cheesy Mashed Potatoes. Even better than Fresh Mashed Potatoes are the cheesy ones. Boil 7 peeled and cut-up medium-sized potatoes in water to cover until very tender, 10-15 minutes. Pierce with a knife to test.

In the meantime, process 6 tablespoons low-fat cottage cheese and 6 tablespoons skim milk in a blender until very smooth.

Drain the potatoes and mash. Pour in the cottage cheese-milk mixture and continue to mash until the potatoes are fluffy and creamy.

I like them just plain, but you can add 1/4 teaspoon cayenne pepper, or 1 tablespoon dried parsley flakes, or 1 teaspoon dried basil. If you have some Roast Beef gravy, pour that over and serve. This makes 7-8 servings.

STUFFED SWEET POTATO

Yield: 1 serving

1 medium-size sweet potato
1/4 medium-size apple, peeled and chopped
1 tablespoon apple juice concentrate
1 tablespoon skim milk
1/4 cup raisins (golden ones, if you can find them)

Microwave Directions

Prick the potato and microwave on high for 6-7 minutes.

Take a slice off of the side of the potato and set the potato cut side up. Scoop out the contents and place in a small bowl. Mix in the other ingredients. Spoon the potato mixture into the potato shell and bake on high for 3 minutes.

Oven Directions

Prick the potato and bake 1 hour in a 350 degrees F. oven.

Take a slice off the side of the potato side and set the potato cut side up. Scoop out the contents and place in a small bowl. Mix in the other ingredients. Spoon the potato mixture into the potato shell and bake for about 15 minutes in a preheated 350 degree F. oven.

BROCCOLI SQUASH COMBO

Yield: 2-3 servings

This recipe sounds very simple, but it is a good example of great taste combinations with no need for extra seasoning, not even pepper.

2-1/2 cups chopped broccoli
1 medium-size white scalloped bush squash (patty pan), cubed
2 tablespoons sapsago cheese

Combine the broccoli and squash in a large pot. Add about 1 inch of water and cover. Boil on medium high heat for 5-7 minutes. Drain. Save the water for soup.

When cooled, process the vegetables with the chopping blade of a food processor or chop very finely with a knife.

Put in a casserole dish and sprinkle with the sapsago cheese. Bake at 350 degrees F. until heated through, about 15 minutes.

CABBAGE EXTRAVAGANZA

Yield: 3-4 servings

1 cup unsweetened pineapple juice
2 tablespoons brandy
1 tablespoon apple juice concentrate
1/3 cup raisins
1 large onion, chopped
8 cups red cabbage cut in chunks (1/2 good-sized red cabbage)
1 teaspoon low-sodium tamari or soy sauce
1/4 teaspoon cayenne pepper or more
1 teaspoon dried basil
2/3 cup chopped apple (1/2 medium to large apple)

In a 5-quart pot, combine the pineapple juice, brandy, and apple juice concentrate. Add the raisins and onion. Bring to a boil, cover, and cook over high heat for 5 minutes. Add the cabbage and sprinkle with tamari or soy sauce and cayenne. Stir and toss all the ingredients together.

Cover, reduce the heat to medium low, and cook until the cabbage is fairly tender, about 3 minutes. Watch the cabbage carefully as it cooks; stir often. It burns easily. Add the basil and cook for 2 minutes. Add the apple chunks and cook for 5 minutes more. Serve.

COLLARDS AND CARROTS

Yield: 3-4 servings

Well, I'm not going to do without my soul food, even if I can't put ham in it. Collard greens are pretty bland without the ham, but I found carrots perk them up and make them taste very good. Collards are very high in calcium and vitamin A, and contain lots of roughage.

1 large onion, coarsely chopped
Water
8 cups chopped collard greens
3 large carrots, sliced
1/4 teaspoon cayenne pepper or more

Place the onion in a nonstick 5-quart pot. Turn the heat on high and sauté, stirring constantly, until the onion looks a little brown around the edges and slightly transparent. Add about 1 inch of water to the pot. Place the collard greens, carrots, and cayenne in the pot and cover. Bring to a boil. Cook over medium heat for about 5 minutes, or until tender. Stir and serve.

TURNIPS WITH TURNIP GREENS
• • • • • • • • • • • • • • • • • • •
Yield: 3-4 servings

Here is some more soul food. Some people used to throw away the greens until they found out what good tasty food they are. Tops of radishes and beets are also delicious cooked this same way with onions. Turnip greens are loaded with iron and a good amount of vitamin A.

2 large purple turnips or 4-5 smaller ones, peeled and cubed
*   (2-2-1/2 cups)*
1 large onion, coarsely chopped
1 teaspoon low-sodium tamari or soy sauce
Cayenne pepper
Water
8 cups young, tender turnip greens, destemmed and chopped

Place the turnips in a nonstick soup pot with the onions. Turn the heat on high, sprinkle the tamari and cayenne over the vegetables, and sauté until the onion and the turnips look brown around the edges, 4-1/2 minutes. Add about 1/2 inch of water to the pot. Add the greens and cover. Cook over medium heat for about 10 minutes, or until tender. Stir occasionally, and add more water if the greens begin to dry out.

Serve along with black-eyed peas over brown rice and Baked Chicken, or Oven-Fried Catfish, or Breaded Pork Chops.

MUSTARD GREENS

• • • • • • • • • • • • • • • • • • • •

Yield: 2 servings

Fresh mustard greens taste superior to canned or frozen ones, and they really aren't that much trouble to fix. Washing them is the biggest problem. I hold a bunch by the stems and dunk them up and down in a large pot of cold water.

2 medium-size onions, chopped
8 cups fresh mustard greens, destemmed and chopped
2 medium-size carrots, sliced
Water
1/8 teaspoon red pepper flakes

Put the onions in a large nonstick soup pot, and turn the heat on high. Sauté until they look a little brown around the edges and somewhat transparent. Add about 1/2 inch water to the pot. Add the greens and carrots and sprinkle the red pepper over them. Cover and cook over medium heat for 10 minutes, or until the greens and carrots are tender. Stir and serve. Save the cooking water for soup.

RED CABBAGE WITH TURNIPS

• • • • • • • • • • • • • • • • • • •

Yield: 4 servings

1 small to medium-size purple turnip, diced
1 medium-size onion, chopped
1 teaspoon low-sodium tamari or soy sauce
1/8 teaspoon cayenne pepper
1/2 medium-size red cabbage, chopped (substitute green cabbage
    if necessary)
3/4 cup water

Combine the turnip, onion, tamari or soy sauce, and cayenne in a nonstick 5-quart pot. Turn the heat on high and saute' the vegetables, turning them over and over until the onions and turnips are pretty brown, 4-1/2 minutes. Add the cabbage and sauté with the other vegetables for about 5 minutes. Add the water, cover, bring to a boil, and cook for about 3 minutes or until the cabbage is tender. Stir every minute. Add more water if the pot starts to dry out. Serve at once.

SUMMER VEGETABLE COMBO

Yield: 2-3 servings

Green beans are the most challenging vegetable to make tasty without salt. But in this recipe they pick up flavor from the other vegetables and are surprisingly good.

2 large carrots
1 small early white bush scalloped squash (Patty Pan)
1 cup fresh or frozen French-style green beans
Water
1 large fresh tomato
1/4 cup chopped fresh parsley

Don't peel anything. Just cut everything up. Put the carrots, squash, and green beans in a large pot with about 1/2 inch of water and cover. Steam over a high heat for about 7 minutes. Then add the tomato and parsley and cook for 1 or 2 minutes more. Mix and serve immediately.

INDIAN CORN WITH PEPPERS

Yield: 2-3 servings

This is an American Indian recipe from the Southwest. Marvelously simple. Tantalizingly good.

1-1/2 cups fresh or frozen corn
Water
1 (4-ounce) can green chili peppers, drained, rinsed, and chopped

Microwave Directions

Place the corn in a 1-quart container. Add 2 tablespoons water. Cover. Heat on high for 3 minutes. Stir in the chili peppers. Cover. Heat on high for 2-3 minutes more, until the corn is tender. Serve hot.

Stove Top Directions

Place the corn in a saucepan with 1/2 cup water. Bring to a boil, cover, and cook for 2 minutes. Add the chili peppers. Cook for 2-3 minutes, until the corn is tender. Serve hot.

STEWED EGGPLANT

Yield: 3-4 servings

Stewed eggplant is a typical Creole delight, and one of the first dishes I learned to cook. I will never forget my surprise the first time I cut into a raw eggplant and saw how firm it was. I had only seen them cooked before, and they are very sloppy and soft when cooked. Rice to sop up the gravy is a must with this.

1 medium-size onion, chopped
1 small green pepper, chopped
1 (16-ounce) can whole tomatoes (do not drain) or 2-2-1/2 cups
   chopped fresh tomatoes
1 cup water
1 large eggplant, peeled and cubed
1 teaspoon dried parsley flakes or 3 tablespoons chopped
   fresh parsley
1/2 cup apple juice concentrate
1/8 teaspoon cayenne pepper
1/2 teaspoon powdered or crumbled thyme
Cooked brown rice (page 233)

Place the onion and green pepper in a nonstick pot. Turn the heat on high and saute' until the onion looks brown around the edges and a little transparent, and the green pepper begins to look a little shiny. Add the tomatoes and the water. Break up the canned tomatoes with a spoon. Add the eggplant and all the remaining ingredients and stir. Cover and cook over medium heat until the eggplant is very tender, 20-25 minutes. Stir often while cooking, and make sure it doesn't burn.

Serve over brown rice. A small piece of steak and some steamed carrots taste good with this.

BROILED PICKLED CUCUMBERS

Yield: 2-3 servings

1 large cucumber
Italian Salad Dressing (page 184)

Peel the cucumber and slice it into 1/2-inch slices. Place in a bowl and cover with the salad dressing. Marinate for at least 2 hours. Drain, reserving the dressing for a salad.

Place the cucumber slices on a nonstick pan. Broil for 5 minutes or until heated through. Serve as a side dish with oven-fried fish or chicken or with a meatless meal for some real taste interest.

SPINACH FLORENTINE

• • • • • • • • • • • • • • • • • •

Yield: 4-6 servings

3 (10-ounce) packages frozen chopped spinach (6 cups)
4 egg whites, slightly beaten
1/2 teaspoon Tabasco sauce
2 teaspoons low-sodium tamari or soy sauce
4 tablespoons grated sapsago cheese
3/4 cup bread crumbs (Pritikin or any other acceptable bread)
Cayenne pepper
Nutmeg

Microwave Directions

Place the frozen spinach in a 1-quart or 1-1/2-quart baking dish. Cover and microwave on high for 8 minutes. Stir. Microwave on high for 8 minutes more. Stir. Remove. Drain and leave the spinach in the baking dish.

Stove Top Directions

Place the spinach in a saucepan with 1 cup water, cover, and cook over medium heat for 3-4 minutes after the water comes to a full boil. Drain and place in a 1-quart or 1-1/2-quart baking dish.

Add the egg whites, Tabasco, tamari or soy sauce, and 2 tablespoons of the cheese to the cooked spinach. Mix well. Mix the remaining 2 tablespoons cheese with the bread crumbs. Sprinkle on top of the casserole. Bake at 350 degrees F. for 30 minutes. Sprinkle cayenne and nutmeg on top and serve.

You can freeze this whole or divided into single portions. To re-heat 1 serving, add 1 teaspoon of water to the bottom of the dish, cover, and heat. To reheat the whole casserole, add 4 teaspoons of water, cover, heat. Although this dish tends to dry out if you don't eat it right away, the water moistens it and brings it back to life.

CREAMED BROCCOLI WITH
MUSHROOMS AND CARROTS

• • • • • • • • • • • • • • • • • • • •

Yield: 3-4 servings

The simple cream sauce enhances the flavor of the slightly cooked vegetables to create a dish nice enough for company. Double everything except the water for steaming to make more servings.

2-1/2 cups chopped fresh broccoli
1-1/4 cups sliced fresh mushrooms
1 medium-size carrot, sliced
1 celery rib, chopped
1/4 cup chopped fresh parsley, loosely packed
1 medium-size onion, chopped
1-1/2 cups water
2/3 cup skim milk
3 tablespoons whole wheat flour
1/8 teaspoon red pepper cayenne
Grated sapsago cheese (optional)

Place all the vegetables in a large pot and add the water. Cover and bring to a boil. Cook for 4-5 minutes. Drain the vegetables and put them in a serving dish. Save the cooking water for soup.

While the vegetables are cooking, pour the milk in a blender with the flour and pepper. Blend until smooth. Pour the mixture into a saucepan on the stove and turn the heat on high. Stir constantly until the mixture thickens. It will be quite thick. Add it to the cooked vegetables and toss to coat them. Sprinkle a little sapsago cheese over each serving, if desired. Serve immediately.

BAKED TOMATO

• • • • • • • • • • • • • • • • • • •

Yield: 2 servings

Serve this with just about everything. It makes a pretty delicious decoration for any plate.

1 medium-size to large tomato
Lemon juice
Cayenne pepper
1 tablespoon grated sapsago cheese

Cut the tomato in half horizontally and remove the stem. Place on a baking pan and squirt a little lemon juice over each half. Then sprinkle on a little cayenne. Sprinkle half the sapsago cheese on each tomato half. Place on the bottom shelf in the oven and bake at 400 degrees F. for 15 minutes. Then place under the broiler and broil for 3 minutes. Serve hot.

CRANBERRY BAKED SQUASH

● ● ● ● ● ● ● ● ● ● ● ● ● ● ● ● ● ● ●

Yield: 2 servings

1 medium-size acorn squash
1/4 cup water
1/4 cup apple juice concentrate
1 tablespoon cornstarch
1 cup cranberries

Microwave Directions

Prick the squash in several places and bake, uncovered, on high in a microwave for 10 minutes.

Cut in half the long way and remove the seeds.

Oven Directions

Prick the squash in several places and place in an oven. Bake at 350 degrees F. for about 30 minutes.

Cut in half the long way and remove the seeds.

In a saucepan, combine the water and juice concentrate. Mix in the cornstarch until the lumps are removed. Cook over medium heat until the mixture thickens and is almost transparent, stirring constantly. Mix in the cranberries.

Divide the cranberry mixture between the two halves of the squash, filling the cavities.

Place the squash halves on a nonstick baking pan and bake at 350 degrees F. for 30-35 minutes, until the cranberries are nice and soft.

This tastes very good served along with Oven-Fried Chicken and Scalloped Potatoes.

Variation

Blueberry Baked Squash. Substitute 1 cup of blueberries for cranberries. Bake at 350 degrees F. for about 10 minutes to heat through.

CREAMY BAKED ONIONS

• •

Yield: 4-5 servings

This dish is lovely with baked fish and boiled or mashed potatoes.

3 medium-size uncooked fish heads
3-1/2 cups water
2 cups or 1 (10-ounce) carton fresh pearl onions
1/4 cup whole wheat flour
1/3 cup skim milk
8 tablespoons whole wheat or Pritikin bread crumbs (1/2 cup)
1/4 teaspoon powdered or crumbled thyme
1/2 teaspoon turmeric
1/8 plus 1/16 teaspoon cayenne pepper
2 teaspoons orange juice concentrate
3 egg whites
Orange slice
1/8 teaspoon paprika Parsley

When you go to the fish market, ask for some fish heads. Trout heads are the right size. Put the heads in a saucepan and cover with the water. Bring to a boil, then simmer uncovered, until the liquid reduces to 2 cups, about 20 minutes. Strain the liquid into a measuring cup, and add water, if necessary to make 2 cups. Discard the fish heads, or give them to your cat.

Peel the onions and keep them wet in a bowl of water to keep yourself from crying. If they start to irritate your eyes while you are peeling them, dunk them again.

Boil the onions in the fish stock over medium heat, covered, until tender, about 15 minutes. Add the flour, sprinkling a tablespoon at a time over the top and mixing it in. Then add the milk, 6 tablespoons of the bread crumbs, the thyme, turmeric, cayenne, and orange juice concentrate. Mix well and let it thicken as you stir over medium heat. Pour all into a small (less than a quart) casserole.

Beat the egg whites with a fork until foamy and pour on top. Sprinkle with the remaining 2 tablespoons bread crumbs. Then sprinkle with paprika. Bake at 400 degrees F. for 20 minutes.

Garnish the top with an orange slice and a little sprig of parsley. Sprinkle a little paprika over the orange, if desired.

VEGETABLES THAT NEED NO HELP

Some vegetables taste so good in their natural state that they need no spices or special way of cooking to taste good. The vegetables that follow are at their best if they are simply steamed. You don't have to cook them to death, just cook until they are tender. I find most cook best in a covered pot with a little water on top of the stove. I will give microwave directions for those that can be cooked successfully that way. Save the cooking water, except from artichokes and spinach, for soup stock.

Artichokes.	Set 2 or 3 artichokes in 1 inch of water in a covered 5-quart pot. Bring to a boil and reduce the heat to low. Cook, covered, for about 25 minutes, until you can pull off a leaf easily and the meat at the base of the leaf is tender.
Asparagus.	Cut off the tough blunt ends, put in a saucepan and pour in enough water to almost cover them. Bring to a boil, cover, and cook over medium heat for 8-10 minutes, until tender.
Brussels sprouts.	I really like these best cooked on top the stove, but they are acceptable done in a microwave. *Microwave Directions:* Place about 2 cups of brussels sprouts in a 1-1/2-quart container with 1/2 cup water. Cover. Microwave on high for 5 minutes. Stove Top Directions: Place about 2 cups of brussels sprouts in a 1-1/2-quart saucepan. Add about 1/2 inch of water. Cover and bring to a boil. Cook on a medium heat for 8-10 minutes, until tender.
Carrots.	Do not peel. Scrub well and cut in desired shapes. *Microwave Directions:* Place the carrots in a 1-1/2-quart container. Add about 1/4 inch of water, cover, and microwave for 5 minutes on high. Stove Top Directions: Place the carrots in a saucepan and add about 1/4 inch of water. Cover and bring to a boil. Cook

over medium heat for about 5 minutes.

Cauliflower.

Steam the whole head in about an inch of water in a covered pot over medium heat for 10-15 minutes. Test with a sharp knife to see if it is done. Or cut the florets off the cauliflower, and place in a saucepan. Add about 1/4 inch of water, cover,and bring to a boil. Then cook over medium heat for about 5 minutes, until tender.

Corn on the cob, fresh or frozen.

Microwave Directions: Place the corn in a plastic bag and leave the end open. Microwave on high for about 1 minute for each piece of corn. If the corn was frozen solid to start, feel the centers to see if they are still cold. If so, microwave a few more minutes. *Stove Top Directions:* Use a large enough pot to hold the corn and add enough water to cover all the ears. Bring the water to a fast boil. Drop the corn in and boil for about 6 minutes.

Green peas, fresh or frozen.

Microwave Directions: Place about 2 cups of peas in a 1-1/2-quart container. Add 1/4 cup water and cover. Microwave on high for 5 minutes. *Stove Top Directions:* Place about 2 cups of peas in a 1-1/2-quart saucepan. Add 1/2 cup of water. Bring to a boil, cover, and cook over medium heat for 5 minutes.

Spinach.

Combine 8 cups of spinach with 1/2 inch of water in a covered pot. Bring to a boil, cover, and cook over medium heat for 8-10 minutes. Drain immediately.

Yellow crook-necked squash.

Cut 2-3 squash into chunks and place in a 1-1/2 quart saucepan. Add 1/2 cup water. Bring to a boil, cover, cook over medium heat for

	5-6 minutes. If you want the squash cut in thin slices, cook whole for 5-6 minutes in 1/2 cup water, then slice. They get too watery if you cut them first.
Zucchini.	Cut the zucchini in big chunks; no need to peel. *Microwave Directions:* Place the pieces in a shallow baking dish. Add 1 tablespoon water. Cover and microwave on high for 5-6 minutes. *Stove Top Directions:* Place pieces in a 1-1/2-quart saucepan. Add 1/2 cup water. Bring to a boil and cover. Cook over medium heat for 5-6 minutes.

You can mix vegetables and cook them together. Nice combinations are:

Broccoli, cauliflower, and mushrooms
Brussels sprouts, carrots, and mushrooms
Carrots and yellow squash
Cauliflower, broccoli, zucchini, and yellow squash
Peas, carrots, and corn
Peas, carrots, and mushrooms
Yellow squash and zucchini
Yellow squash, zucchini, and mushrooms

White scalloped bush squash, sometimes called Patty Pan, is a little bland by itself, but cut up and mixed with carrots and zucchini it really tastes good. Green beans are also bland without the benefit of salt or butter, but they taste good mixed with carrots, corn, and cabbage.The mixed vegetables look pretty too. As long as each vegetable has about the same cooking time, it is easy to mix them together.

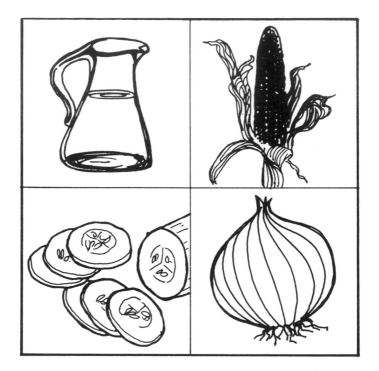

CHAPTER 8

SALADS

SALADS ARE REALLY IMPORTANT TO YOUR DIET. YOU CAN EAT just about all you want. Most of the time you will be thinking of lettuce, tomatoes, and cucumbers, perhaps a few onion rings. Watercress makes a great addition to any fresh salad, when you can find it. Experiment with different greens, such as rocket or arugula, mache, and lamb's quarters. If you see some unusual vegetables at the grocery that look like they would be good In a salad, try them out. You don't need a special recipe for a fresh green salad.

Some of the dressings that last a long time, such as Vinaigrette, Greek, and Italian, I make by the quart or so, and store in the refrigerator.

When you get tired of fresh green salads, try some of the other recipes in this chapter. I tried to make these salads fun to make, as well as fun to eat.

VINAIGRETTE DRESSING

Yield: About 1-1/3 cups

This sounds simple, but it is no slouch of a dressing. My husband just raves about it everytime I use it.

1/2 cup wine vinegar
2 tablespoons apple juice concentrate
3/4 cup water
1/16 teaspoon cayenne pepper

Mix ingredients well and serve. Store extra in the refrigerator.

GREEK DRESSING

● ●

Yield: 1 cup

The grape juice and coriander in this make the dressing especially Greek tasting. People wonder what is in it, but they can never put their finger on it. The color is that of a good wine vinegar.

1/2 cup apple cider vinegar
1/2 cup water
2 tablespoons grape juice concentrate
4 coriander seeds
1/16 teaspoon ground ginger
1/16 teaspoon curry powder
1/16 teaspoon cayenne pepper

Combine the ingredients in a blender and blend until the coriander seeds have disappeared. Serve. Store extra in the refrigerator.

ITALIAN SALAD DRESSING

● ● ● ● ● ● ● ● ● ● ● ● ● ● ● ● ● ● ●

Yield: 1-1/2 cups

Italian Salad Dressing is an all-purpose dressing that tastes great on any fresh green salad. It has a special affinity for tomatoes.

1 cup apple cider or wine vinegar
1/2 small onion
1/4 cup water
1/4 cup apple juice concentrate
1/2 teaspoon garlic powder or 4 garlic cloves
1/2 teaspoon onion powder
1/2 teaspoon dried basil
1/2 teaspoon dried oregano
1/8 teaspoon cayenne pepper
1/4 teaspoon cumin

Combine all the ingredients in a blender and liquify. Serve. Store extra in the refrigerator.

FRESH TOMATO DRESSING

Yield: 2 servings

1 medium-size ripe tomato
2 tablespoons apple cider vinegar
2 whole canned green chili peppers
1 teaspoon dried onion flakes

Place all the ingredients in a blender and liquify. Delicious over Senorita Salad (page 190), lettuce and tomatoes, or any other fresh salad fixings.

SOUR CREAM DRESSING

Yield: 2 servings

1/2 cup low-fat cottage cheese
1/4 teaspoon Tabasco sauce
1/2 small onion, cut in pieces

Combine the ingredients in a blender or food processsor and process until smooth. Pour over salads. Use at once. This does not keep well.

IMITATION MAYONNAISE

Yield: 1/2 cup

This does not taste exactly like mayonnaise, but it is pretty close. It does have the tanginess and sweetness that mayonnaise has. It doesn't keep very long, perhaps a day or two, so don't make more than you need for one meal.

1/2 cup low-fat cottage cheese
1 teaspoon finely chopped onion
1 teaspoon apple juice concentrate

Combine the ingredients in a blender or food processor and blend or process until smooth. Double, triple, or quadruple the amounts if needed.

B & B DRESSING

• •

Yield: 1 cup

The first "B" stands for beans and the last "B," believe it not, stands for bananas. Puree beans and they are very creamy. The banana adds creaminess, richness, and the sweetness. The curry helps to blend all the flavors. Just trust.

1/2 cup cooked lima beans (page 91)
1/4 cup cider vinegar
1 teaspoon grapefruit juice concentrate
2 tablespoons orange juice concentrate
1/2 cup sliced banana, firmly packed
1/16 teaspoon curry powder
1/8 teaspoon cayenne pepper

Put all the ingredients in a blender and blend until very smooth. Serve over a green salad.

This does not keep well. You can use extra dressing twice the same day — mix again before using.

PLANTATION DRESSING

• •

Yield: 1 cup

1 cup skim milk yogurt (page 224)
1/8 teaspoon cayenne pepper
15 coriander seeds
1/16 teaspoon allspice
1/2 medium-size banana
2 teaspoons grated sapsago cheese

Combine the ingredients in a blender and blend until the coriander seeds are pulverized. Serve all at once. Do not save any leftovers.

CAYMAN ISLANDS DRESSING

• •

Yield: About 1-1/2 cups

1/2 plus 1/3 cup skim milk yogurt (page 224)
1 medium-size banana, broken up

1/2 cup cubed apple
1 tablespoon fresh lime juice
1 penny-size piece lime rind
1/8 teaspoon cayenne pepper

Combine all the ingredients in a blender. Blend until smooth.

OLD-FASHIONED SALAD
• • • • • • • • • • • • • • • • • • • •
Yield: 2 servings

1 medium-size cucumber, sliced
3 small green onions, including green parts, sliced
1/8 cup thinly sliced white cooking onion
Vinaigrette Dressing (page 183)
1 medium-size tomato, diced
5 romaine lettuce leaves

Combine the cucumber, green onions, and white onion rings with the dressing. Marinate in the refrigerator for at least 2 hours.

When you are ready to serve, drain the vegetables and reserve the dressing. Mix the diced tomatoes with the cucumber and onions. Tear up the lettuce and distribute over 2 salad plates. Place the mixed vegetables over the lettuce and pour on some of the dressing. Save the rest of the dressing for another salad. By this time it will have taken on a wonderful taste from the onions and cucumbers.

PICKLED CUCUMBERS
• • • • • • • • • • • • • • • • • • • •
Yield: 1-2 servings

1 medium-size cucumber
Apple cider vinegar
1 teaspoon onion powder
1 teaspoon garlic powder

Peel and cube the cucumber. (Peeling is optional; I think these taste better peeled.) Cover the cucumber cubes with apple cider vinegar and sprinkle the onion powder and garlic powder on top. Mix. Let sit overnight in the refrigerator. Pour off the vinegar and save it to pour over salads. Add the pickled cucumber cubes to salads, sandwiches, or eat as they are.

PETER RABBIT SALAD

• •

Yield: 2 large or 4 small servings

22 fresh or frozen snow pea pods
1 medium-size onion
5 radishes
1 medium-size carrot
1 small turnip
1/4 cup chopped green pepper
1 cup coarsely chopped fresh parsley
3 small green onions, including green parts
1 celery rib
1 large tomato
4 slices Pritikin or commercial whole wheat bread
7 or 8 romaine lettuce leaves (more if needed), torn into
    bite-size pieces
1/2 cup low fat-cottage cheese (use 1 cup for 4 salads)
1 carrot (for the rabbit)
1 cup Plantation Dressing (page 186)

If you use the fresh snow peas, break off the ends and wash them.

This is where your food processor can shine. Slice the onion in rings and the radishes very thinly. Change to the grater blade and grate 1 carrot and the turnip. Chop the green pepper by hand. Barely chop the parsley at all, just get rid of the stems. Slice the celery and dice the tomato. Toss all the vegetables.

Remove the crusts from the bread and slice into cubes. Place them on a cookie sheet in a preheated 400 degree oven F. for 3-4 minutes, until they are brown and toasted, but not burned. Set aside.

Place the lettuce leaves on 2 dinner plates or 4 salad plates. When you are ready to serve, toss the croutons with the vegetables and divide the salad between or among the plates. Put 1/4 cup of cottage cheese on top of each salad. Peel a carrot and cut a section about 2 1/2 inches long. Cut it in 4 sections the long way. Lay a section on top of the cottage cheese on each salad with the cut side of the carrot up. It will look like a whole small carrot. Pour the dressing over each salad and serve.

SNOWPEA SALAD

Yield: 2 servings

3 ounces or about 28 snow pea pods, fresh or frozen
1/8 cup very thinly sliced white cooking onion
2 radishes, thinly sliced
1 small yellow squash, thinly sliced
1 celery rib, sliced 1/8 inch thick
Vinaigrette Dressing (page 183)
1/4 cup curly parsley, destemmed
4-5 romaine lettuce leaves
1 large tomato, in wedges

If you use fresh snow peas, cut off the ends and ragged tips. Toss together the snow peas, onion, radishes, yellow squash, and celery. Add the dressing and marinate for 2 hours.

When ready to serve, drain and reserve the dressing. Toss the parsley with the marinated vegetables. Tear up the lettuce leaves and arrange on 2 salad plates. Layer the tomato wedges over the lettuce, then place the marinated vegetables over the tomatoes. Pour on some dressing. Serve.

COLE SLAW A LA TROPIQUE

Yield: Six 1/2-cup servings

This is a good one to serve at a luau or on a winter day when you wish you could be snorkling in warm, crystal clear, blue green water off a tropical island in the West Indies.

2-1/2 cups shredded cabbage
1/2 cup finely chopped carrot
1/2 cup raisins
1/3 cup chopped red bell pepper
1/4 cup finely chopped onion
1 medium-size sliced banana
1 recipe Cayman Islands Dressing (page 186)

Toss together all ingredients and serve. If you want to stretch this recipe, add a little more cabbage.

FULL MEAL SALAD

Yield: 2 servings

1/2 cup fresh peas, steamed, or frozen green peas, defrosted
1/2 head iceberg lettuce
10 tomato slices
1/2 cup cucumber slices
2 radishes, sliced
1 cup cubed boiled potatoes
1/2 cup alfalfa sprouts
1/2 cup sliced mushrooms
1/2 cup sliced celery
1/2 medium-size green pepper, chopped
1/2 cup low-fat cottage cheese
1/2 cup grated carrot
1 cup B & B Dressing (page 186)

Divide the lettuce between 2 dinner plates. Layer the tomato slices over the lettuce. Layer the cucumber and radishes. Layer the cubed potatoes. Place the alfalfa sprouts in a bunch right in the middle of each salad. Layer the mushrooms over each salad. Next layer the celery, then the green pepper. Put a 1/4-cup mound of low-fat cottage in the center of each salad. Arrange the grated carrot around each cottage cheese mound like a nest. Sprinkle the peas over the salad. Use B & B Dressing.

SENORITA SALAD

Yield: 2 large or 4 small salads

1/2 cup thinly sliced white onion
1 cup sliced cucumber
1 cup diced tomatoes
2 cups cooked garbanzo beans (chick-peas) (one 15-ounce can)
1 cup coarsely chopped fresh parsley, loosely packed
Lettuce
Fresh Tomato Dressing (page 185) (double the recipe)

Place the onion, cucumber, and tomatoes in a bowl. Drain and rinse the garbanzo beans. Add them to the bowl with the parsley and toss. Serve over beds of lettuce and top with the dressing.

SOCRATES SALAD

• •

Yield: 2 large servings or 4 small servings

The sliced red bell pepper makes this especially nice, but greens ones will do if you can't get the red ones.

2 cups firmly packed fresh spinach leaves
1/2 cup alfalfa sprouts (optional)
1/2 medium-size cucumber, sliced
6 radishes, sliced
1 cup button mushrooms, sliced
1/2 cup sliced red bell peppers
3 small green onions, including green parts, sliced
Greek Dressing (page 184)

Lay the spinach on 2 dinner plates or 4 salad plates. Layer alfalfa sprouts on top, then the cucumber slices, radish slices, mushroom slices, red bell pepper slices, then green onions. Pour on the dressing and serve.

MARDI GRAS SALAD

• • • • • • • • • • • • • • • • • • • •

Yield: 4-5 servings

The colors in this salad remind me of Mardi Gras.

1 large tomato, cubed
3/4 cup sliced yellow squash
1 cup shredded red cabbage
1 cup unpeeled, sliced purple turnip
1/2 cup sliced radishes
1/4 cup sliced carrots
1 medium-size onion, sliced very thinly
3/4 cup sliced cucumber
1/4 cup coarsely chopped fresh parsley
Red leaf lettuce
Vinaigrette Dressing (page 183)

Toss all the ingredients together except the lettuce and dressing. Make beds of lettuce on salad plates and place the rest of the salad on top. Pour the dressing over and serve.

ARTICHOKE SALAD

● ●

Yield: 2 servings

Lettuce
5-6 canned artichoke hearts or 2 large fresh cooked or canned
  artichoke bottoms
3/4 cup fresh or frozen peas
Sour Cream Dressing (page 185)

Arrange the lettuce on 2 salad plates. Cut the artichoke hearts in half and distribute over lettuce. Or, if you have artichoke bottoms, place one on each plate. Artichoke bottoms are extremely nice for this as they make cups for the peas, but they are hard to find canned. Do not use artichokes canned or bottled in oil. Use the frozen peas right out of the package. You might want to cook fresh ones for just a minute or two in a little water in a covered saucepan. Spoon the peas over the artichokes. Top with the dressing and serve.

MOLDED FRUIT SALAD

● ●

Yield: 16-18 servings

This makes a lovely fruit salad for a buffet dinner. I serve this to a crowd every New Year's Day along with cabbage for money, black-eyed peas for good luck, and roast beef. I used to serve corned beef, but that is a little too fatty for these days.

3 cups orange juice
1 (20-ounce) can unsweetened pineapple chunks and juice
1 (16-ounce) can unsweetened grapefruit sections and juice
1 cup apple juice or cider
1/2 cup apple juice concentrate
3 envelopes unflavored gelatin
1 (12-ounce) carton low-fat cottage cheese (1-3/4 cups)
Kumquats or orange slices and parsley

Pour the orange juice, the pineapple chunks and juice, and grapefruit sections and juice into a 3-quart ring mold.

Bring the apple juice and apple juice concentrate to a boil in a saucepan. Remove from the heat and add the gelatin, stirring to dissolve the gelatin. Pour into the mold with the other ingredients and mix. Refrigerate for about 4 hours, until solid.

To unmold the salad, immerse the mold in hot water for several seconds. Place a large serving plate on top of the mold. Turn the whole thing over. The salad should fall right onto the plate. Remove the mold. If it doesn't unmold, run a knife around the edges and place in the hot water again. Repeat if it still doesn't unmold.

Fill the center of the mold with the cottage cheese. Garnish around the sides and top with kumquats and leaves. Or use curly parsley and halved orange slices.

The taste is rather tart. If you like a very sweet taste, replace the grapefruit juice with the same amount of apple juice concentrate.

SCHEHERAZADE PASTA SALAD
• • • • • • • • • • • • • • • • • •
Yield: 2 large or 4 small servings

1 cup raw rotini twist macaroni, whole wheat or semolina
1/4 cup fresh or frozen peas
1/2 cup diced carrot
1/2 cup diced yellow squash
1 medium-size cucumber, sliced
1/4 cup or 3 small green onions, sliced
1/4 cup chopped celery
1/4 cup chopped fresh parsley
1/3 cup chopped unsweetened dates
Lettuce
1 recipe Cayman Islands Dressing (page 186)

Bring a quart of water to a boil and pour in the macaroni. Boil semolina noodles for 9 minutes, whole wheat noodles for about 15 minutes. Drain, pour cold water through, and drain again. Set aside.

If the peas are fresh, place in a saucepan with about 1/2 inch of water and bring to a boil. Cover and boil for 2 minutes. Drain and cool. Use frozen peas straight out of the package.

Mix together the macaroni, peas, carrot, squash, cucumber, onions, celery, parsley, and dates.

Arrange the lettuce on salad plates. Place the salad mixture over the lettuce, pour on the dressing, and serve

CARROT SALAD SUPREME

Yield: 4-5 servings

1-1/2 cups grated carrots, lightly packed (3 large carrots)
1 celery rib, chopped
1/2 cup raisins
Imitation Mayonnaise (page 185)
2 teaspoons apple juice concentrate
1/16 teaspoon cayenne pepper
1/16 teaspoon curry powder
Lettuce

Mix the carrots with the celery and raisins.

Prepare the Imitation Mayonnaise in a blender or food processor. Add the juice concentrate, cayenne, and curry powder. Blend or process. Mix the Imitation Mayonnaise with the carrots, raisins, and celery. Serve over beds of lettuce on salad plates.

POTATO SALAD

Yield: 9-10 servings

8 medium-size potatoes
1 large onion, coarsely chopped
4 celery ribs, coarsely chopped
Pickled Cucumbers (page 187)
4 hard-boiled egg whites, chopped
1 (12-ounce) carton low-fat cottage cheese (1-3/4 cups)
1/2 large onion
2 garlic cloves
1 teaspoon Tabasco sauce

Boil potatoes in water to cover for 15-20 minutes, until soft. Drain then cool. Peel and cube. Combine potatoes with onion, celery, cucumbers, and egg whites. Combine cottage cheese and 1/2 of the large onion, garlic, and Tabasco sauce. Blend until smooth. Pour over potatoes and toss. Serve cold.

SUMMER FRUIT SALAD

• • • • • • • • • • • • • • • • • • • •

Yield: 4 servings

1 cup diced watermelon
1 cup diced cantaloupe
1/2 cup seedless grapes
1/2 cup sliced peaches
1/2 cup sliced bananas
1/2 cup sliced strawberries
1/2 cup sliced kiwi fruit (optional)
Cayman Islands Dressing (page 186)
Lettuce (optional)

Toss all the fruits together. Exact amounts of fruits are not necessary. The measures given are just to provide an idea of about how much to use. Ladle into fruit cups or prepare a bed of lettuce on salad plates and spoon the fruit on top. Pour some dressing over each salad and serve.

STRAWBERRY MOUNTAIN

• • • • • • • • • • • • • • • • • •

Yield: 2 servings

1/2 cup fresh, frozen, or sugar-free canned chopped peaches
1 cup low-fat cottage cheese
2 tablespoons apple juice concentrate
2 cups bite-size pieces iceberg lettuce
1/2 cup fresh or frozen sliced peaches
1 cup whole fresh or frozen strawberries
1/4 cup water

Combine the chopped peaches with the cottage cheese and 1 tablespoon of the juice concentrate. Place lettuce on 2 salad plates. Mound cottage cheese on the center of each plates on top of the lettuce. Place the peach slices around cheese. Place one whole strawberry on top of each mound. Arrange the rest of the strawberries around the bottom of the mounds on top of the peaches. Mix the remaining 1 tablespoon of the juice concentrate with the water and pour over the salads, making sure to get some on the lettuce leaves. Serve.

CHAPTER 9

DESSERTS

I WANT TO WARN YOU. THESE DESSERTS DO CONTAIN CALORIES. A slice of the blueberry pie (about one sixth of a pie) contains about 230 calories.

That's about as bad as a slice of traditional apple pie. The difference is you are eating stuff that is really good for you instead of things that are going to hurt you: sugar (lots of it), fat (lots of it), and refined flour.

I suggest that if you are going to eat a dessert, incorporate it into your diet plan for the day. For instance, you could consider the topping of the blueberry pie as a milk serving, the Grape-nuts® crust as a bread serving, and the blueberries, banana flakes, and apple juice as a fruit serving. It might not be exact, but it is close to the right amount for each serving.

These desserts are nice for bringing along to potluck dinners. Then you have something you can eat, and no one will suspect it is diet food. I brought my blueberry pie to a potluck dinner one night, and it was as well received as the gorgeous cheesecakes, rum cakes, and other full-of-sugar-and-butter cakes. No one even suspected they were eating something that was good for them.

A friend of mine was at the party, and she looked very sad. She moaned, "I can't eat one thing here tonight." She was on a special diet and could not eat anything that contained salt, fat, or sugar. I announced, "Oh yes, you can eat something here tonight!" "No I can't." she answered pitifully. I insisted, "Yes, you can. Come see." I took her hand and led her to the dessert table and showed her the pie. She said, "I can't eat that. What's in it?" As I told her, her eyes grew big and she practically yelled, "I can eat it! I can eat it!" She was so happy I thought she was going to cry. She got a dinner plate and served herself a really big piece. Well, she considered it her dinner.

LEMON CREAM PIE

● ●

Yield: One 9-inch pie

Cream Pie Topping (page 204)
Basic Dessert Pie Crust (page 204)
4-1/2 lemons
3/4 cup apple juice concentrate
3/4 cup water
4-1/2 tablespoons cornstarch

Prepare the Cream Pie Topping according the recipe directions, and refrigerate for 3-4 hours, or overnight. Don't beat it until you are ready to spread it on the pie.

Prepare the pie crust according the recipe directions and set aside.

Squeeze the lemons and pour the juice into a saucepan. Add the juice concentrate and water. Add the cornstarch and stir until the mixture is smooth. Cook over medium heat, stirring constantly, until the mixture is thickened and looks transparent. Pour into the pie shell. Cool in the refrigerator for about a half hour.

When the pie has cooled, beat the Cream Pie Topping according to the recipe directions. Spread it on top. Refrigerate for at least 2 hours before serving. A lemon slice on top makes a nice garnish.

BLUEBERRY CREAM PIE

● ● ● ● ● ● ● ● ● ● ● ● ● ● ● ● ● ● ● ●

Yield: One 9-inch pie

If you double this recipe, it fits very nicely into a 9-inch by 13-inch baking dish for serving a crowd.

Cream Pie Topping (page 204)
Basic Dessert Pie Crust (page 204)
1 cup apple juice concentrate
1/4 cup water
3 tablespoons cornstarch
2 cups fresh or frozen blueberries, plus a few extra

Prepare the Cream Pie Topping according to the recipe directions, and refrigerate for 3-4 hours, or overnight. Don't beat it until you are ready to spread it on the pie.

Prepare the Basic Dessert Pie Crust according to the recipe directions and set aside.

Pour the juice concentrate and water in a saucepan. Add the cornstarch and stir until smooth. Cook over medium heat, stirring constantly, until it starts to thicken. Continue to stir rapidly. When it begins to look transparent, remove from heat. Fold in the blueberries and pour into the pie shell. Smooth around to fit. Set aside.

When the pie is cool, beat the Cream Topping and spread it over the top. Drop a few blueberries over it for decoration. Chill for about an hour before serving.

BLACKBERRY PIE

● ● ● ● ● ● ● ● ● ● ● ● ● ● ● ● ●

Yield: One 9-inch pie

Things have certainly changed. Now, I have to go out in the woods and pick my own blackberries. When I was a kid in New Orleans, old peddlers would come around the neighborhood singing "Blaaaak Berrieee!" It was wonderful. We could buy pints of blackberries when they were in season. But I haven't seen anybody selling blackberries in years. I guess it isn't so bad though, because we have turned blackberry picking into a family event combined with crawfishing. The crawfish and the blackberries are in season at the same time and in the same places, so while we wait for the crawfish to climb into our nets, we hunt for the berries. They make a delicious pie, the blackberries, that is; well the crawfish do too, now that I think of it.

Basic Dessert Pie Crust (page 204)
4 cups blackberries
1 cup apple juice concentrate
3 tablespoons cornstarch

Prepare the pie crust according to the recipe directions. Bake at 400 degrees F. for 5 minutes. Set aside.

Simmer the blackberries in the apple juice concentrate until they are limp. Place the cornstarch in a small saucepan. Drain off the berry liquid into the saucepan containing the cornstarch, slowly stirring all the time. When the mixture is smooth, cook over a medium heat until it thickens, stirring constantly. Add the blackberries. Stir, then pour into the pie shell. Cool and serve.

PUMPKIN PIE

• • • • • • • • • • • • • • • • • • • •

Yield: One 9-inch pie

Basic Dessert Pie Crust (page 204)
1-1/2 quarts raw pumpkin, loosely packed
1/2 cup water
1 medium-size ripe banana
1/4 cup apple juice concentrate
1/4 cup raisins (golden if you can find them)
1/4 teaspoon nutmeg
1/4 teaspoon ginger
1/4 teaspoon cinnamon
1/4 teaspoon mace
1/2 teaspoon allspice
2 tablespoons banana flakes
1 teaspoon vanilla extract
6 egg whites

Prepare the crust in a 9-inch pie pan. Set aside.

Microwave Directions

Place the pumpkin in a 2-quart container and add 1/2 cup of water. Cover and cook on high for 12 minutes.

Stove Top Directions

Place the pumpkin in a pot large enough to hold 2 quarts or a little more. Add 1/2 cup of water. Cover and bring to a boil. Reduce the heat to medium-low and cook for 10-12 minutes. Check every 4 or 5 minutes and stir.

When the pumpkin is tender, pour off the water to use in a soup or gravy. It's really great in chicken or turkey gravy. Let the pumpkin cool a little and then place it in a blender or food processor. Add the banana, apple juice concentrate, raisins, spices, banana flakes, vanilla, and egg whites. Blend until all trace of the raisins disappears. Pour into the crust. Bake at 375 degrees F. for 45 minutes. Cool before serving.

To prevent the crust from burning around the edges, place an aluminum foil circle over the crust edge after the first 15 minutes of baking. If it won't lay down, use aluminum pellets or weights (available from gourmet kitchen shops) to weigh it down.

Depending on the size eggs you use and how fresh they are, you will come out with more or less pie filling. Sometimes the eggs froth up so much you will have almost enough to fill 2 pies. Make a second crust if you do. With 6 egg whites, you will always have enough to fill at least 1 crust.

STRAWBERRY CREAM DESSERT
• • • • • • • • • • • • • • • • • • •
Yield: 8-9 servings

Cream Pie Topping (page 204)
Basic Dessert Pie Crust (page 204)
1 envelope unflavored gelatin
1/2 cup water
1/2 cup apple juice concentrate
3 cups sliced fresh or frozen strawberries

Prepare the Cream Pie Topping according to the recipe directions and refrigerate for 3-4 hours, or overnight. Don't beat it until you are ready to spread it on top of the pie.

Prepare the pie crust according to the recipe directions and set aside.

Soften the gelatin in 1/4 cup of the water. Combine the remaining 1/4 cup water and juice concentrate in a saucepan and bring to a boil. Remove from the heat, and add the gelatin and water. Mix until the gelatin dissolves. Cool.

Add the strawberries (reserving a few for garnish) to the cooled gelatin mixture. Place the strawberry mixture in the refrigerator and chill until slightly gelled. Pour into the crust and chill until firm, about 2 hours.

Beat the Cream Pie Topping according to the recipe directions and spread on top. Garnish with a few whole strawberries. Chill for 1 hour before serving.

CHEESECAKE

• • • • • • • • • • • • • • • • • • •

Yield: 8-9 servings

When I first made this cake, my 16-year-old boy, Guillaume, said "Mama, this is an excellent cheesecake." I was thrilled. Coming from a 16-year-old, that is the highest compliment I have ever been given about my cooking. He proceeded to eat most of the cake, but I managed to save one piece for his daddy.

Cake

Basic Dessert Pie Crust (page 204)
1 (12-ounce) carton low-fat cottage cheese (1-3/4 cups)
3/4 cup drained crushed canned unsweetened pineapple
1/4 cup banana flakes
1 1/2 teaspoons vanilla extract
1/2 teaspoon cinnamon
3/4 cup apple juice concentrate
2 envelopes unflavored gelatin

Topping

1 (13-ounce) can evaporated skim milk
1 envelope unflavored gelatin
1/4 cup banana flakes
1 teaspoon vanilla extract
Stawberries, pineapple chunks, blueberries

Prepare the pie crust according to recipe directions. Press into an 8-inch by 8-inch cake pan or baking dish. Bake at 350 degrees F. for 10 minutes. Cool.

Cream the cottage cheese in a blender or food processor at a low speed. Add the pineapple, banana flakes, vanilla, and cinnamon and blend.

Mix the juice concentrate with the gelatin in a saucepan and let sit for 3 minutes. Bring to a boil, remove from the heat, and stir to dissolve the gelatin. Let cool, then add to the cottage cheese in the blender or food processor and blend. Pour over the baked crust. Refrigerate.

To make the topping, mix 1/2 cup of the milk with the gelatin and banana flakes. Let it sit until the gelatin softens. Heat the remaining milk. When the gelatin and banana flakes are soft, add the heated milk and stir to dissolve. Add the vanilla. Cool.

Pour the mixture into the blender and blend until very, very smooth. Place in a mixing bowl. Cover with plastic wrap and have the wrap touch the milk so it does not harden on top. Place in the refrigerator for about 4 hours, or until gelled.

Beat with an electric cake mixer, starting at a low speed and building up to the highest speed. Mix until smooth and fluffy. Spread over the top of the chilled filling. Garnish with strawberries, pineapple chunks, or blueberries or a little of each, if you like. Refrigerate for about 2 hours before serving.

TUTTI FRUTTI TREAT
• • • • • • • • • • • • •   • • • • •
Yield: 8-9 servings

Basic Dessert Pie Crust (page 204)
2 medium-size apples
1/2 cup raisins
1/2 cup frozen or fresh blueberries
1/4 teaspoon cinnamon
1-1/4 cups apple juice concentrate
1/4 cup water
3 tablespoons cornstarch

Prepare the pie crust according to the directions. Press into an 8-inch by 8-inch cake pan and set aside.

Peel and core the apples; cut into small chunks and distribute over crust. Distribute the raisins and blueberries over the apple pieces, reserving a few blueberries for a garnish. Sprinkle cinnamon over the top and cover with aluminum foil. Bake for 40 minutes at 350 degrees F. Remove from the oven, but leave the foil on while you prepare the topping.

Pour the juice concentrate and water into a small saucepan. Add the cornstarch and stir well until the mixture is smooth. Cook over high heat, stirring constantly. Keep stirring and suddenly the mixture will begin to thicken. When it does, continue stirring rapidly until mixture looks practically transparent. Pour it immediately over the pie and smooth it around. Garnish with about 20 or so raw or frozen blueberries.

This can be eaten immediately, but it tastes much better if it is refrigerated for at least a few hours before serving.

CREAM PIE TOPPING

Yield: Enough to top 1 pie

You won't believe how creamy and good this topping turns out. This alone may keep you on your diet. It takes the place of whipped cream.

1 (13-ounce) can evaporated skim milk
1 envelope unflavored gelatin
1/4 cup banana flakes

Pour about 2 inches of milk in a cup and sprinkle the gelatin and banana flakes over it to soften. Stir well.

Meanwhile, scald the rest of the milk in a microwave on high for 5-1/2 minutes or on top of the stove. Remove any skin that forms on top of the milk.

Add the rest of the milk mixed with the gelatin and banana flakes. Stir well. Let it cool a little and then pour the mixture into a blender. Set on liquify or high and blend until very smooth. Pour into a mixing bowl and cover with plastic wrap. Let the wrap touch the top of the milk to keep the gelatin from forming a hard skin on top. Refrigerate for 3-4 hours until gelled.

When it has gelled, beat with an electric mixer. Start slowly, building up to the fastest speed. Beat until the mixture is fluffy and creamy. Spread on top of a prepared pie.

BASIC DESSERT PIE CRUST

Yield: One 9-inch pie crust

1-1/2 cups Grape-nuts cereal
1/4 cup apple juice concentrate

Pour the Grape-nuts into a nonstick 9-inch pie pan. Add the juice and stir until the Grape-nuts are moist. Press into the pan to form a crust the shape of the pan. Set aside while you make the filling.

BAKED APPLE WITH RAISINS

• •

Yield: 1 serving

1 medium-size apple
Raisins
1/2 teaspoon Poiret Pear and Apple Spread

Core the apple and try not to punch a hole in the bottom. Fill the cavity with raisins. Put the half teaspoon of the pear and apple spread on top.

Microwave Directions

Microwave on a serving dish for 2 minutes on high.

Oven Directions

Put the apple on an ovenproof serving dish. Bake, uncovered, at 350 degrees F. for 1 hour.

Serve warm.

HOLIDAY FRUITCAKE

Yield: About 16 servings

When you buy dried fruit, make sure it contains no honey or sugar. If you can't find one of the fruits, substitute an equal amount of raisins.

2 tablespoons chopped lemon rind
2 tablespoons chopped mandarin or regular orange rind
1/2 cup brandy
3/4 cup plus 1 tablespoon apple juice concentrate
1-1/2 cups dried pineapple
1-1/4 cups raisins
1/2 cup dates
1/4 cup dried pears
1/2 cup prunes
3/4 cup dried figs
4 egg whites
1-1/2 teaspoons vanilla extract
1/8 teaspoon baking soda
1-1/4 cups whole wheat flour

Combine the lemon and mandarin rinds in a mixture of 1/4 cup brandy and 1/4 cup of the juice concentrate. Marinate this mixture in the refrigerator for a few days before you start the cake. You can chop up all the dried fruit at this time, and put it in a plastic bag or a plastic-covered container. No need to refrigerate.

When the day comes to assemble your cake, combine the egg whites, the remaining 1/2 cup plus 1 tablespoon juice concentrate, the reserved brandy/rind/juice concentrate mixture, the vanilla, and baking soda in a large bowl. Mix well. Sift the flour over the mixture and mix it in until smooth. Then mix in the chopped fruit. Mix it all very well.

Spray an 8-inch by 5-inch loaf pan with a nonstick spray and pack the mixture in. Set the cake on the middle rack in the center of a preheated 275 degree F. oven and bake for 2-1/2 hours. A toothpick inserted in the center should come out clean.

When the cake is done, remove it from the oven and turn it out onto a cake rack to cool. You might have to loosen it with a knife. If some of it sticks to the bottom of the pan, just scrape it off and pat it back firmly onto the bottom of the cake.

When the cake is cooled, turn right-side-up onto a cake plate. Poke holes all over the top of the cake with a toothpick. In a metal measuring cup or a very small saucepan, pour in the remaining 1/4 cup brandy. Hold the cup or pan over a candle until the brandy feels warm, not hot to the touch. Strike a match and hold over the top of the brandy and it will flame immediately. If it doesn't, heat it a little longer. Let it flame until it goes out. Use an eyedropper or just dribble the brandy over the cake and let it soak in as it goes. Cover with aluminum foil and let it sit for 48 hours before serving.

Keep portions small to stay within Pritikin dried fruit guidelines.

BANANA RAISIN PUDDING

• • • • • • • • • • • • • • • • • •

Yield: 4-5 servings

2 cups skim milk
1/4 cup cornstarch
4 ripe bananas
1 cup raisins
1-1-1/2 cups fresh or frozen blueberries
1 teaspoon vanilla extract

Combine the milk and cornstarch in a blender and process until smooth. Add 3 of the bananas, cut in chunks, and blend.

Microwave Directions

Pour mixture into a 5-cup glass container. Add raisins. Cook uncovered on medium. Cook 14 minutes, stirring every 3 minutes. Before the last 2 minutes, slice and add the last banana. Stir in.

Stove Top Directions

On top of the stove, put water in the bottom of a double boiler and pour the milk mixture into the top part. Add the raisins. When the water on the bottom begins to boil, start stirring the pudding and continue stirring until it thickens. When it is pretty thick, slice and add the remaining banana and cook a little more, 2-3 minutes.

Cool slightly and stir in the vanilla. Pour into pudding glasses or custard cups, leaving a little room at the top. Just before serving, garnish generously with frozen or fresh blueberries. The blueberries really make this recipe because they add just the right amount of tartness.

CANTALOUPE ICE CREAM

• • • • • • • • • • • • • • • • • • •

Yield: 1-2 servings

12 ice cubes
1-1/2 tablespoons low-fat cottage cheese
1/4 cup banana flakes (or a little more to taste)
1 cantaloupe slice, 1-1/2 inches thick
Red seedless grapes

Place the ice cubes in a food processsor and process until the ice is pulverized. Add the cottage cheese, banana flakes, and cantaloupe. Process again until everything is pulverized. Don't add too many banana flakes, or it will make the mixture dry, and don't process too long as the mixture will become watery.

This makes 1 very large serving or 2 smaller ones. Garnish with red seedless grapes and serve immediately.

To double the recipe, make only 1 batch at a time. It goes fast, and if you chill the glasses first, the other servings will remain frozen until you get them all done. The smaller-size servings will fit in champagne glasses.

Extra servings can be frozen. Ten minutes before serving, remove from the freezer to soften. Break up the ice cream, and combine in a blender with 2-3 tablespoons skim milk. Process briefly until creamy and serve.

VARIATION

Blueberry Ice Cream. Substitute 1/3 cup or a little more of frozen blueberries for the cantaloupe. I like the frozen ones because they are full of ice and don't melt the mixture as fast as the fresh ones.

CANTALOUPE CAROB ICE CREAM

• • • • • • • • • • • • • • • • • • •

Yield: 1-2 servings

This is extra special with the peppermint extract added. It is so cooling on a hot summer day, I make it quite often. It's all right to binge on this. Carob powder is naturally sweet.

12 ice cubes
1-1/2 tablespoons low-fat cottage cheese

1/4 cup banana flakes (or a little more to taste)
1 cantaloupe slice, 1-1-1/2 inches thick
3 tablespoons unsweetened carob powder
1/8-1/4 teaspoon peppermint extract (optional)
Red or green seedless grapes

Place the ice cubes in a food processor and process until the ice is pulverized. Add the cottage cheese, banana flakes, cantaloupe, carob powder, and peppermint extract. Process again until all is pulverized. Don't add too many banana flakes or it will make the mixture dry, and don't process for too long or it will make the mixture watery. Garnish with either red or green seedless grapes.

This recipe will fill 2 champagne glasses. To double it, make a separate batch. The 2 filled glasses will stay frozen while you make the second batch, if you have everything cut up, measured, and ready to put in the food processor.

Extra servings can be frozen. Ten minutes before serving, remove from the freezer to soften. Break up the ice cream, and combine in a blender with 2-3 tablespoons skim milk. Process briefly until creamy and serve.

GRAPEFRUIT REFRESHER

• • • • • • • • • • • • • • • • • • •

Yield: 2 cups

This is a really delicious way to get your vitamin C and some roughage, too. If you are used to having alcohol in the evening, this will reduce your craving for it, I guarantee.

1 fresh grapefruit
10 ice cubes
Juice of 1/2 lemon
1/4 cup apple juice concentrate
1/2 cup sparkling mineral water

Dig out the grapefruit sections and place them in a blender. Add the juice from the grapefruit, too. Add the ice cubes, lemon juice, juice concentrate, and mineral water. Blend until the ice is crushed. Pour in 2 tall glasses over more ice cubes and drink. Yum!

FRESH FRUIT FIRENZE

• • • • • • • • • • • • • • • • • • •

Yield: As many servings as you like

Desserts don't have to be elaborate to be good. A simple dessert of fresh fruit can be elegant and delicious.

When Ray and I were in Florence, Italy, a few years back, we were on a street that everyone walks down to go from the Piazza del Duomo to the Piazza della Signoria, called the Via Dei Calzaiuoli. The Piazza del Douomo is the one with the cathedral with the big dome and the baptistry that has the gold carved doors by Lorenzo Ghiberti, which Michelangelo called "the door to paradise." If you go to Florence (Firenze as they call it there) you will find it right away.

The Piazza della Signoria is the one you see in all the movies with the pigeons and the big reproduction of Michelangelo's statue of David. It's the largest in Florence. Well, more or less; it is certainly the most entertaining.

We were hot, tired, and thirsty from walking, so about halfway between the two piazzas we went into a little café. It was on the left coming from the Duomo. I don't remember any doors, so it was open air in feeling.

Served there was the most refreshing fruit dessert I have ever tasted. They mixed fruits and covered them with watermelon juice. It was very well chilled and tasted great on a hot day. I felt air conditioned after eating that dessert.

I make a dessert at home I call Fresh Fruit Firenze; it tastes just like that memorable dessert in Florence.

Watermelon
Cantaloupe
Seedless grapes
Peach chunks
Watermelon juice to cover fruit
Apple juice concentrate (optional)

Use equal parts of each fruit and cut into bite-size pieces. Use the seedless part of the watermelon for the dessert. Then cut up the pieces of watermelon that have the most seeds and put them in a colander. Set the colander over a bowl and with a potato masher, mash the watermelon to extract the juice. After mashing some,

---

with very clean hands, squeeze the remaining juice from the watermelon. Pour into the bowl with the fruit. It should almost cover the fruit. If you don't have enough, add some water and apple juice concentrate to make enough. Use very ripe fruit so this will taste sweet. Add apple juice concentrate if your fruit turns out to be not very sweet. Chill for at least 1 hour before serving. If you want, serve with a scoop of Cantaloupe Ice Cream over the top.

STRAWBERRY FRAPPE
• • • • • • • • • • • • • • • • • • • •
Yield: 1-2 servings
With a strawberry drink this good, who needs rum?

5 large fresh or frozen strawberries
5 ice cubes
2 tablespoons apple juice concentrate
2 tablespoons water

If you use frozen strawberries, do not defrost them. Put all the ingredients in a blender and blend until the ice is pulverized. Serve immediately.

BANANA FRAPPE
• • • • • • • • • • • • • • • • • • •
Yield: 2 servings

1 large banana
1/2 cup skim milk
8 ice cubes
2-3 drops almond extract (optional)

Peel and freeze the banana. Then place it in a blender with the milk, ice cubes, and almond extract. Blend until the ice is pulverized. Serve at once.

CHAPTER 10

SNACKS, DIPS, AND TIDBITS

WHERE WOULD THIS WORLD BE WITHOUT SNACKS AND FUN foods?

Keep some Mock Sour Cream or some Creole Cream Cheese on hand in the refrigerator with cut up vegetables for dipping. Measure the dip and count it as your milk serving for that day. You don't have to give up popcorn. It is very easy to make without oil. Grapefruit sweetened with a little apple juice concentrate makes a very refreshing snack, as well as a fruit serving. A microwave baked banana is really delicious and satisfying.

If you keep legal snacks on hand, they will keep you from going for the no-no's. I always take some popcorn and fruit with me in my car when I leave the house, along with a thermos of hot or iced herb tea, so I won't be tempted to stop for a hamburger or a soft drink.

This chapter will help prepare you for the tempting times.

BANANA SNACK

Yield: 1 serving

1/2 ripe banana
1 tablespoon water

Take half of a banana cut the short way. Place on a saucer and pour water over. Microwave for 1-1/2 minutes on high, or until it looks flat and collapsed. For variety, sprinkle several raisins over the banana before cooking.

POPCORN

• • • • • • • • • • • • • • • • • • • •

Yield: 1 serving

1/4-1/3 cup raw popcorn

Microwave Directions

Pour 1/3 cup popcorn into a small brown paper bag. Twist the top lightly to let steam escape, leaving lots of room for the corn to pop. Microwave on high for 3-1/2 minutes. Serve.

Stove Top Directions

Put 1/4 cup porcorn in a small nonstick pot with a handle and cover. Turn the heat on high. When it starts to heat up, shake the pot often. After a minute or two, when you hear it starting to pop, shake constantly until you don't hear any more popping. Pour in a bowl. Let it cool a little, and it will become light and fluffy.

Some people like to shake onion powder or garlic powder on popcorn. I don't care much for it, but it's worth a try.

ARTICHOKE DIP

• • • • • • • • • • • • • • • • • • •

Yield: About 1-1/2 cups

Put this in a hollowed-out cabbage and place big cabbage leaves under the cabbage head. Place fresh vegetables for dipping around on the big leaves. It will look really beautiful.

4 artichoke hearts canned in water, or 4 cooked frozen
   artichoke hearts, or 2 cooked artichoke bottoms from
   fresh artichokes
1 (12-ounce) carton low-fat cottage cheese (1-3/4 cups)
1/4 teaspoon Tabasco sauce

Drain and rinse canned artichokes.

Spoon the cottage cheese into the blender. Spoon the artichokes on top. Start blending on a slow speed. After it gets going a little, stop and push the artichokes down. When everything is well-blended, add the Tabasco, and switch to high speed for about a minute. Or mix in a food processor fitted with a cutting blade. Just throw everything in and process until smooth.

MOCK SOUR CREAM OR ONION DIP

Yield: 1-3/4 cups

This mixture is so versatile it can be used for a dip, as mayonnaise, potato topping, and topping for many dishes in this book.

1 (12-ounce) carton low-fat cottage cheese (1-3/4 cups)
1 small onion
1 teaspoon Tabasco sauce
1 tablespoon skim milk

Place all the ingredients in a blender or food processor and process until the cottage cheese is smooth. It doesn't blend easily, so if it looks as if it is just sitting there, stop the machine and push the cheese around some. Eventually it will all get going. Store extra in the refrigerator.

CREAMY FRUIT DIP

Yield: About 2-1/2 cups

This dip is lovely for placing on a tray with sliced cantaloupe, strawberries, apple slices, pineapple chunks, and, perhaps, carrots, celery, or other fruits or vegetables that could be dipped. Be sure to coat apple slices with lemon juice so they don't turn brown.

1 (12-ounce) carton low-fat cottage cheese (1-3/4 cups)
3/4 cup drained unsweetened canned crushed or chopped
    fresh pineapple
1-1/2 teaspoons vanilla extract
1/2 teaspoon cinnamon
3-4 tablespoons banana flakes (optional)

Place all the ingredients, except the banana flakes, in a blender and blend on a low speed until the cheese is creamy. Taste. The dip will not be extremely sweet. Consider, though, that the fruit you will be dipping will be sweet. However, if you would like it sweeter, add the banana flakes a tablespoon at a time and blend until it is sweet enough for you.

MOCK STUFFED EGGS

- - - - - - - - - - - - - - - - - - - -

Yield: 16-18 servings

8-9 eggs
1/2 medium-size cucumber
Apple cider vinegar
1-1/2 teaspoons onion powder
1/2 teaspoon garlic powder
2 cups cooked garbanzo beans (chick-peas) (one 15-ounce can)
1/8 teaspoon curry powder
1/2 teaspoon Tabasco sauce
Paprika

Place the eggs in cold water to cover. Bring the water to a boil. Reduce the heat to medium and boil for 10 minutes. Remove from the heat and cool in cold water.

While the eggs boil, peel and cut the cucumber into very small morsels. Place the cucumber in a bowl with 1 teaspoon of the onion powder, 1/4 teaspoon of the garlic powder, and enough apple cider vinegar to cover. Stir to mix in the garlic and onion. Marinate until you are ready to mix them with the garbanzo beans; 5-6 minutes is enough, but if you wish, you can fix them a day ahead and let them marinate overnight. They taste about the same either way.

Drain the garbanzo beans and rinse to remove as much salt as possible. Put the drained beans in a food processor. Add the curry powder, the remaining 1/4 teaspoon garlic and 1/2 teaspoon onion powder, the Tabasco sauce, and 1 teaspoon of vinegar. Process until very creamy.

When the eggs are cooled, peel and slice them in half the long way. Remove the yolks and discard or give them to your dog or cat.

Drain the cucumber and mix with the garbanzos. Stuff the mixture into the egg halves. Sprinkle with a little fresh paprika to garnish.

CUCUMBER SANDWICHES

- - - - - - - - - - - - - - - - - - - -

Yield: 4 finger sandwiches

1/4 cup low-fat cottage cheese
1 tablespoon finely chopped onion
1/4 teaspoon red hot sauce (not Tabasco)

1/2 teaspoon chili powder
1 tablespoon chopped fresh parsley
1/4 cup thinly sliced cucumber
2 slices Pritikin or commercial whole wheat bread

Mix together the cottage cheese, onion, hot sauce, chili powder, and parsley. Spread the mixture on one slice of the bread. Top with the cucumbers. Cover with the other slice of bread. Cut off the crusts and slice into 4 party-size sandwiches.

PICKLED PEARL ONIONS
• • • • • • • • • • • • • • • • • • •
Yield: 4 cups

Measure the ingredients exactly because if you are off just a little, the onions won't taste right. They will be too sour or too sweet.

1 cup water
1/4-1/2 teaspoon of red pepper flakes (use more if you like
    the heat)
7/8 cup vinegar
3/4 cup apple juice concentrate
20 ounces or 4 cups raw unpeeled pearl onions

Combine the water, red pepper, vinegar, and juice concentrate in a saucepan. Bring to a boil and boil for 2 minutes. Set aside to cool.

To peel the onions, first put the unpeeled onions in water that is a comfortable temperature for your hands. Remove the onions one at a time to peel. If the one you are peeling starts to irritate your eyes, dunk it to wet it again. As long as the onions are wet, they won't bother your eyes. Trim the root part of the onion. Wash well and pop them into the vinegar mixture. Cover and marinate in the refrigerator for 3-4 days before eating.

Variations

Pickled Mushrooms. Substitute 4 cups button mushrooms for the onions and proceed as directed above.

Pickled Cucumbers. Substitute 4 cups unpeeled cubed cucumber for the onion and proceed as above.

CHAPTER 11

SAUCES, GRAVIES, AND OTHER BASICS

GRAVIES, SAUCES, CREPES: THESE PROVIDE THE EXTRAS THAT make food worth eating. I don't think my husband and I could stay on this program if we didn't have our Roast Beef Gravy, our Brown Turkey Gravy, and our Italian Tomato Sauce. I don't have a brown chicken gravy in this chapter because I get chicken gravy from the recipe for Country Chicken Stew.

MEDITERRANEAN SAUCE

• • • • • • • • • • • • • • • • • •

Yield: 1-1/2 cups

This delicious sauce was intended to go over Crab Quiche but it is also great over toast.

1 cup Concentrated Chicken Stock (page 58)
1/2 cup sliced green onions, including the green part
(6 small ones)
1 tablespoon unbleached flour
1 (13-ounce) can evaporated skim milk
1/2 (6-ounce) can white crabmeat or 1/3 cup packed whitecrab meat
1/8 teaspoon cayenne pepper

Combine the chicken stock and onions in a medium-size saucepan. Boil, uncovered, for 6 minutes, until the liquid has almost disappeared. Quickly, stir in the flour and reduce the heat to medium. Slowly stir in the milk. Cook for 4 minutes, stirring constantly. Add the crabmeat and cayenne and cook for 1 minute more. Serve immediately.

DESSERT CREPES

• • • • • • • • • • • • • • • • • • • •

Yield: 6 crepes

1 cup whole wheat flour
2 teaspoons low-sodium baking powder
2 egg whites
1/3 cup apple juice concentrate
1 cup water
1 teaspoon vanilla extract

Mix together the flour and baking powder. Add egg whites, concentrate, water, and vanilla. Mix in a blender or food processor.

Pour a little cooking oil on a paper towel. Rinse the towel under the faucet, then wring it out. Wipe it around the surface of a nonstick frying pan. Place the pan on medium heat to preheat it.

Pour 1/3 cup of the batter into the pan. Immediately tilt the pan in all directions so the batter will spread. When the top of the crepe starts to bubble all over, see if the bottom is getting a little brown at the edges. When it starts to brown, flip the crepe. I find the easiest way to do this is to coax the crepe up on one end with a spatula. Grab the lifted edge of the crepe with your finger and thumb; it shouldn't be that hot. Push underneath the crepe with the spatula as you pull up with your fingers. When the spatula is halfway underneath, you should be able to lift and turn the crepe over.

If you are an experienced crepe or pancake maker you can cook these on a high heat, which I usually do, and they go much faster.

When the second side is about half as brown as the first side it is done. Lift the crepe out and place it on a hot plate and do another one. If the crepes start to stick, wipe the pan again with the wet paper towel. Place finished crepes on a hot plate.

You can double this recipe and freeze the extras. Place plastic wrap between each crepe. Reheat frozen crepes in a microwave stacked at least 2 high for about 1 minute. To reheat in the oven, stack them at least 2 high on an ovenproof dinner plate covered lightly with aluminum foil. Heat in an oven preheated to 350 F. for 5-6 minutes. A toaster oven is not good for heating these. Because the crepes are very thin, they become too crisp.

CREPES

• • • • • • • • • • • • • • • • • • •

Yield: 6 crepes

3/4 cup unbleached white flour
1/4 cup oat bran cereal or 1/4 cup unbleached flour
2 teaspoons low-sodium baking powder
1-2/3 cups skim milk
2 egg whites

Mix together the flour, oat bran, and baking powder. Add the egg whites and skim milk and mix in a blender or food processor.

Pour a little cooking oil on a paper towel. Rinse it under the faucet, then wring it out. Wipe it around the surface of a nonstick frying pan before you start and repeat every third crepe.

Preheat the pan for just a few minutes on high. Pour in 1/3 cup of the batter and tilt the pan in all directions. The batter will spill over and almost fill the bottom of the pan. When the top starts to bubble all over, let it keep cooking for a little longer then try to lift an edge. If it looks like it doesn't want to come up, let it cook a little longer. Sometimes when it is ready to be turned, one edge will curl up a little. The first one is the hardest to cook, so don't despair if you mess it up. When you can get an edge up with the spatula, look under the crepe. If it looks tan, slide the spatula under it and grasp the edge of the crepe with your thumb and forefinger and turn it over with the help of the spatula. This is much easier than flipping it in the air.

Place finished crepes on a hot plate.

You can double this recipe and freeze the extras. Place plastic wrap between each crepe. Reheat frozen crepes in a microwave stacked at least 2 high for about 1 minute. To reheat in the oven, stack them at least 2 high on an ovenproof dinner plate covered lightly with aluminum foil. Heat in an oven preheated to 350 degrees F. for 5-6 minutes. A toaster oven is not good for heating these. Because the crepes are very thin, they become too crisp.

FRUIT PATRICIAN

• • • • • • • • • • • • • • • • • • • •

Yield: 5-6 servings

This makes a refreshing dessert by itself or served over Cantaloupe Ice Cream. Or serve hot over Whole Wheat Pancakes or with Poulet Sauce aux Fruit and brown rice or brown and wild rice.

You can usually find the 16-ounce bags of mixed frozen fruit in the frozen food section of the supermarket. You can also find the 2 kinds of melons mixed in a bag, too. If you can't, just buy bags or packages of the separate fruits and use equal parts of each to make up about 4 cups of fruit in all.

1 (16-ounce) package of frozen mixed fruit (strawberries, grapes, cherries, and pineapple)
1 cup frozen honeydew and cantaloupe
1-1/3 cup water
2 tablespoons cornstarch
1/2 cup apple juice concentrate

Defrost the fruit. Pick out the strawberries and set aside.

Combine the water and cornstarch and stir until smooth. Set aside.

Combine the juice concentrate and all the fruit, except the strawberries, in a 1-1/2-quart saucepan. Bring to a boil. Stir in the cornstarch mixture. Cook, stirring constantly, until the mixture looks transparent and slightly thickened.

If you would like thicker sauce, add another tablespoon of cornstarch and cook a few minutes longer. Add more apple juice concentrate for a sweeter taste. Add the strawberries at the very last minute so they will retain their color.

Remove from the heat and serve, or chill and serve cold.

Variation

Crepes Patrician. Prepare 1 batch of Fruit Patrician and 4 Dessert Crepes. Put 1 crepe on each plate with the first side you cooked facing the plate. Spoon some fruit and syrup on top. Then fold the crepe in half. Pour more fruit and syrup over. To make it really fancy, heat 1/4 cup of brandy in a small container that has a lip for pouring, then set the brandy on fire with a match. After it burns a little, pour some over each crepe and serve at once.

CHERRY GLAZE

Yield: About 3 cups

This glaze is super! You can use it over Cheesecake or over the chicken in Poulet Sauce Cerise, over Cantaloupe Ice Cream, or over Whole Wheat Pancakes, or mixed with Skim Milk Yogurt, or just eat it by itself.

I hope you can find the tart red pitted cherries packed in water at your grocery. If not, drive the manager crazy until some are ordered. It will be worth it.

1 (16-ounce) can tart red pitted cherries, packed in water
Water
1/2 cup apple juice concentrate
1/4 cup orange juice concentrate
1/16 teaspoon allspice
2 tablespoons cornstarch

Drain the cherries and reserve the juice. Put the cherries in a 1-1/2-quart saucepan. Add the juice concentrates and the allspice.

Measure the reserved juice and add water to equal 1-1/3 cups. Add 1 cup of the liquid to the cherries. Combine the remaining 1/3 cup liquid with the cornstarch. Stir until smooth. Set aside.

Bring the cherries to a boil. Stir in the cornstarch mixture. Cook and stir until smooth. Continue stirring for about 4 minutes until the liquid begins to look clearer and thicker.

Let the sauce cool to lukewarm before using over the cheesecake, yogurt, or ice cream.

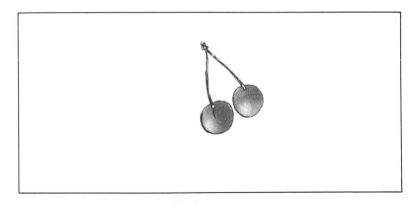

CRANBERRY SAUCE

• • • • • • • • • • • • • • • • • • •

Yield: About 4-1/2 cups

12 ounces fresh or frozen cranberries (4 cups)
1 cup apple juice concentrate
1/2 cup water
1/2 envelope gelatin
1 or more tablespoons banana flakes (optional)

Rinse the cranberries, remove stems and bad berries.

Microwave Directions

Place berries in a 2-quart container. Add the concentrate and water. Microwave, uncovered, 5 minutes on high. Reduce to simmer or low and microwave for 10 minutes. Stir once at half time.

Stove Top Directions

Place the berries in a large saucepan and add the juice concentrate and water. Bring to a boil. Boil, covered, for 5 minutes; then simmer for 10 minutes. Stir often.

Set half of the cooked cranberries aside. Add the gelatin to half the mixture and stir until dissolved. Pour into a blender and liquify. Taste. If you want it sweeter, add 1 tablespoon of banana flakes at a time and blend. Don't add too many, though, or the mixture will become dry. If this happens, add more apple juice concentrate to moisten it. Remove it to a bowl. Refrigerate for 3-4 hours.

When the mixture has gelled, mix it with the remaining whole berries. Refrigerate until you are ready to serve.

HOMEMADE SKIM MILK YOGURT

• • • • • • • • • • • • • • • • • • •

Yield: 1 quart

I cannot tell you the feeling of power I had the first time I made yogurt. There it was after 6 hours, all nice and quivering in little cups. Unbelievable! It's not all that hard and not all that particular, either. The first time, after I got everything together and had it warming up and I was all nervous, I discovered I had added only half of the culture. I was frantic but I let it alone - and it still came out.

Go to the health food store and ask for dry yogurt culture. The next batch can be made with 3 tablespoons of the yogurt you prepared before. You can use the yogurt from the grocery store only if it contains live cultures. After you have made 6 or 7 batches, get a new package of the dry yogurt culture because the yogurt will keep getting tarter and tarter each time.

This is really delicious mixed with Cherry Glaze and in Cayman Islands Dressing and Plantation Dressing.

1 quart skim milk
1 teaspoon plain gelatin
3 tablespoons hot water
3 tablespoons instant nonfat dry milk powder
1 package of dry yogurt culture or 3 tablespoons of the most
    recent batch of yogurt

Scald the milk. Mix the gelatin with the hot water. Remove the milk from the heat and stir in the nonfat dry milk and gelatin. Cool to 90-120 degrees F.; then stir in the culture or 3 tablespoons yogurt. Pour it into a blender and blend. Pour it into 1 cup crocks or small jars or even coffee cups.

Now you have to incubate the yogurt, which means keeping it between 105 degrees F. and 115 degrees F.

Method No. 1

Heat a 5-quart slow cooker on low for 10 minutes. Turn it off. Take a pie pan that will fit inside and turn it upside down in the bottom of the cooker. Cover the cups or jars with aluminum foil and place them in the cooker. Put the cover on and let the yogurt sit for 45 minutes. Turn the cooker on again for 10 minutes on low and turn it off. Keep doing this for 5-6 hours, letting the yogurt sit for 45 minutes between heatings.

Method No. 2

Cover the crocks or cups and place in a gas oven with just the pilot lit. Let sit for 5-6 hours.

Method No. 3

Put the yogurt mixture in crocks or cups and make in an electric yogurt maker. Follow the manufacturer's instructions.

Store the finished yogurt in the refrigerator.

CREOLE CREAM CHEESE

Yield: 2 cups

I had to quit eating Creole Cream Cheese because it contains cream and they don't make a low-fat version. However, I read that if you took yogurt and put it in cheesecloth and placed it in a colander and let it drip, it made some kind of cheese. I couldn't believe the results. It turned out to be Creole Cream Cheese. I use it with baked potatoes. It is also great spread thickly over whole wheat bread. It doesn't hold its shape as well as sour cream, but by itself, or with chopped fresh herbs or garlic or finely chopped onion and a drop or two of tabasco, it makes a delicious dip for fresh vegetables or toasted homemade tortilla chips.

1 quart skim milk yogurt (page 224)

Put a piece of cheesecloth in a colander and place the colander over a bowl. Put the yogurt in it and fold the cheesecloth over the top. Let it sit in the refrigerator overnight. By morning the whey will have dripped out, and there will be Creole cream cheese.

To make a small amount for baked potatoes, I set a coffee filter in an orange juice strainer and put 1 cup of yogurt in it and let it drip. It makes 1/2 cup. You can use the whey as part of the water needed in making bread for a little different taste and extra nutrition.

CHINESE MUSTARD SAUCE

Yield: 2 servings

2 teaspoons dry mustard
1 tablespoon water

Mix together the mustard and water until smooth. This makes enough for two.

SWEET AND SOUR SAUCE

● ● ● ● ● ● ● ● ● ● ● ● ● ● ● ● ● ● ●

Yield: 2 servings

4 teaspoons Poiret Pear and Apple Spread
1-1/2 teaspoons apple cider vinegar
1 teaspoon water

Mix all the ingredients together until smooth and serve.

MOCK KITCHEN BOUQUET

● ● ● ● ● ● ● ● ● ● ● ● ● ● ● ● ● ● ●

Yield: About 1/4 cup

I feel funny about using store-bought Kitchen Bouquet because it has caramel in it. So I turned to the method used by Creole cooks on the plantations in the South.

When cooks used a fireplace or hearth in kitchen buildings that were separate from the plantation houses, they used to thrust a whole onion, no doubt attached to a skewer, skin and all, into the burning coals. When it began to brown, they would remove it, dust off the ashes, and toss it into a soup or gravy.

Peel of 4 onions
Water
1/4 teaspoon garlic powder
1/2 teaspoon onion powder
1 tablespoon apple juice concentrate

Peel the onions and wash the peels if they look dirty. Dry them. Line a cookie sheet with aluminum foil and crimp the edges. Place the peels on the cookie sheet on the bottom rack of the oven. Bake at 500 degrees F. for 10 minutes. Check the peels. Let them bake until just before they turn almost black.

Place the browned onion peels in a small saucepan. Cover with water and boil until the liquid has reduced by about three quarters. Strain the remaining liquid into a cup or bowl and add the garlic powder, onion powder, and juice concentrate.

This extract is somewhat bitter, so add 3 tablespoons more of concentrate to take the bitterness out.

ROAST BEEF GRAVY I

Yield: 3-4 cups

It is hard to predict exactly how much gravy this will make, because sometimes the meat is full of juice and sometimes it is rather stingy about producing a generous amount of drippings. It is quite possible you will end up with more than 4 cups. I freeze the gravy in small amounts and keep for adding to other recipes, such as Italian Tomato Sauce. It adds meat flavor without the meat.

4-5 pound eye of round or rump roast
2 cups beef stock or water
5 tablespoons whole wheat flour
2 tablespoons onion flakes
1/2 cup chopped fresh parsley
3-4 fresh mushrooms, sliced (optional)
Mock Kitchen Bouquet (page 227)
2-3 tablespoons apple juice concentrate
2 bay leaves
1/2 teaspoon powdered or crumbled dried thyme
1/2 teaspoon garlic powder
1/4-1/2 teaspoon cayenne pepper

To make a flavorful gravy, start out with a well-seasoned roast. When you begin, be sure to cut off any visible fat. Either stuff fresh garlic pieces into little holes you make with a knife into the roast or sprinkle with garlic powder. Also sprinkle with onion powder and cayenne pepper. Place the roast in a roasting pan and bake in a preheated oven at 400 degrees F. until the outside is brown. Reduce the heat to 350 degrees F. Bake for 18-20 minutes per pound for a medium rare roast. A meat thermometer registers 175 degrees F. for medium rare, and 180 degress F. for well done. Add 2 inches of water to the pan and roast, uncovered, until the desired doneness is achieved. Baste occasionally. Remove the roast and put the pan of drippings in the refrigerator.

The next day all the grease should be at the top, hardened. Remove and discard the grease.

Place the water or beefstock in a blender and add the flour. Blend. Place the roasting pan with the drippings on the stove, covering 2 burners, if necessary, and add the remaining ingredients and the stock/flour mixture. Bring to a boil and stir until the gravy is thickened.

Slice the roast beef and store in 1-1/2-ounce packages in the freezer for days you can have meat.

If you don't want to use a whole roast for this, you can use about 2 pounds of beef neck bones. Place them in a roasting pan and sprinkle with garlic powder, onion powder, and cayenne pepper. Roast in a preheated 400 degree F. oven. Let them get very, very brown. Add about 2 inches of water and place on top of the stove over 2 burners, if necessary. Simmer, covered, for 30-45 minutes. Add water if necessary to maintain at least an inch of water in the pan. Remove the neck bones and give them to the dog or whatever. There isn't much meat on them. Place the drippings in the refrigerator overnight and proceed with the recipe as directed above.

ROAST BEEF GRAVY II

Yield: 1-1-1/2 cups

4-5-pound eye of round roast
2 garlic cloves, sliced, or 1/2 teaspoon garlic powder
1/4 cup dried onion flakes
Cayenne pepper
4-5 mushrooms
1/4 cup water
2 tablespoons cornstarch

Remove all visible fat from the meat. Place in a slow cooker or a roasting pan. Make small holes in the roast with a sharp knife and stuff fresh garlic slices into them, or just sprinkle the roast with garlic powder. Sprinkle the roast with cayenne pepper and then sprinkle it thickly with dried onion flakes.

Slow Cooker Directions

The very best way to do this is in a slow cooker. Place the roast in the slow cooker and cover. Do not add any water at this time. Turn it on high. When the roast is brown, add about 2 inches of water. Let the roast continue to cook until fully done, about 4 hours. Remove the roast and put the drippings in the refrigerator.

Oven Directions

Place the seasoned roast in a preheated 400 degree F. oven and let it brown. When brown, add about 2 inches of water to the pan. Reduce the heat to 350 degrees F. and roast, basting occasionally, until the desired doneness is achieved. Bake 18-20 minutes a pound for a medium rare roast. A meat thermometer registers 175 degrees F. for medium rare and 180 degrees F. for well done. Remove the roast from the pan and put the drippings in the refrigerator.

The next day remove the grease and discard. Heat the drippings and add the mushrooms. Cook the mushrooms over medium heat until they darken.

Combine the cornstarch with the water. Stir until smooth. Stir into the gravy. Cook over medium heat, stirring all the time, until the gravy thickens. Add a little water if necessary.

BROWN TURKEY GRAVY

Yield: About 4 cups

Drippings and juice from a roasted turkey
2 cups turkey or chicken stock or water
5 tablespoons whole wheat flour
2 tablespoons dried onion flakes
1/2 cup chopped fresh parsley
Mock Kitchen Bouquet (page 227)
3-4 tablespoons apple juice concentrate
1/2 teaspoon dried sage
1/2 teaspoon powdered or crumbled thyme
1/2 teaspoon marjoram
1/2 teaspoon garlic powder
1/4-1/2 teaspoon cayenne pepper

After the turkey is roasted, remove it from the gravy and chill the gravy. The grease will rise to the top and harden. Discard all the grease.

If you are in a hurry to make the gravy for the immediate meal, remove as much grease as possible with a dipper. Then add enough ice cubes to cover the top of the gravy. Stir them around, turning them over; they will collect all the extra grease remaining. Remove the ice cubes.

Add the stock or water. Mix. Add the whole wheat flour and pour all into a blender. Blend and then return to the pot. Add the remaining ingredients and cook over medium heat, stirring all the time until thickened.

If you don't have a fresh roasted turkey, but you do have some rich turkey stock (not too diluted) left from another turkey, you can make the gravy the same way, using the same seasonings.

ITALIAN TOMATO SAUCE

Yield: About 4-1/2 cups

This is most useful to keep on hand as it is used in several recipes. Sometimes I make a double batch to freeze in 1-cup containers.

1 large onion
1 large green pepper
1 medium-size carrot
1 celery rib with leaves
7 large mushrooms
2 cups water
1/2 cup rosé wine
1/2 cup Roast Beef Gravy I (page 228) or II (page 230)
1/2 cup no-salt tomato paste
1 tablespoon grape or apple juice concentrate (preferably grape)
1 teaspoon dried oregano
2 teaspoons dried or 1/2 cup chopped fresh parsley
1/2 teaspoon red pepper flakes
1/2 teaspoon cumin
1/2 teaspoon garlic powder or 5 garlic cloves, chopped
1-1/2 teaspoons dried basil

Chop the onions and green peppers rather coarsely, then chop the carrots and celery very finely, preferably in a food processor. Slice the mushrooms.

Place the vegetables in a nonstick pot and turn the heat on high. Sauté, tossing the vegetables over and over until the onions look brown around the edges and a little transparent. Add the water immediately and stir. Reduce the heat to low. Then add the wine, beef gravy, tomato paste, juice concentrate, oregano, parsley, red pepper flakes, and cumin. Cover and cook on low heat for 2 hours. Check often and stir. Add more water if the sauce starts to become too thick.

If you use fresh garlic, add it 20 minutes before the end. During the last 10 minutes of cooking, add the garlic and basil.

BROWN RICE

• • • • • • • • • • • • • • • • • • • •

Yield: Nine 1/3-cup servings

1 cup uncooked brown rice (preferably long grain)
2 cups water

Microwave Directions

Combine the rice and water in a tall-sided, 2-quart container. (A 2-quart measuring cup is ideal.) Cover and microwave on high for 5 minutes. Reduce to simmer or low and cook for 40 minutes. Allow the rice to sit for 10-15 minutes, covered. Fluff with a fork.

Stove Top Directions

Combine the rice and water in a 2-quart saucepan. Bring to boil, cover, reduce the heat to low, and cook for 40 minutes. Let sit, covered, for 10-15 minutes. Fluff with a fork.

Variation

Brown and Wild Rice. Mix 1 part wild rice with 4 parts brown rice and cook exactly as you would brown rice.

WHITE RICE

• • • • • • • • • • • • • • • • • • • •

Yield: Nine 1/3-cup servings

1 cup uncooked long-grain white rice
2 cups water

Microwave Directions

Combine the rice and water in a tall-sided 2-quart container. (A 2-quart measuring cup is ideal.) Cover and cook in the microwave on high for 5 minutes. Reduce to simmer or low and cook for 15 minutes. Allow the rice to sit for 10-15 minutes, covered. Fluff with a fork.

Stove Top Directions

Combine the rice and water in a 2-quart saucepan. Bring to a boil, cover, reduce the heat to low, and cook for 20 minutes. Let sit, covered, for 15-20 minutes. Fluff with a fork.

INDEX